Cambridge Preliminary English Test 4

WITH ANSWERS

Examination papers from University of Cambridge ESOL Examinations: English for Speakers of Other Languages

CAMBRIDGE
UNIVERSITY PRESS

PUBLISHED BY THE PRESS SYNDICATE OF THE UNIVERSITY OF CAMBRIDGE
The Pitt Building, Trumpington Street, Cambridge, United Kingdom

CAMBRIDGE UNIVERSITY PRESS
The Edinburgh Building, Cambridge CB2 2RU, UK
40 West 20th Street, New York, NY 10011–4211, USA
477 Williamstown Road, Port Melbourne, VIC 3207, Australia
Ruiz de Alarcón 13, 28014 Madrid, Spain
Dock House, The Waterfront, Cape Town 8001, South Africa

http://www.cambridge.org

First published 2003

Printed in the United Kingdom at the University Press, Cambridge

Typeface Helvetica 10/13pt *System* QuarkXPress® [OD&I]

A catalogue record for this book is available from the British Library

ISBN 0 521 75527 1 Student's Book
ISBN 0 521 75528 X Student's Book with answers
ISBN 0 521 75529 8 Teacher's Book
ISBN 0 521 75530 1 Set of 2 Cassettes
ISBN 0 521 75531 X CD Set
ISBN 0 521 75532 8 Self-study Pack

Contents

To the student   4

Test 1   6

Test 2   26

Test 3   46

Test 4   66

Test 1 Key   86

Test 2 Key   99

Test 3 Key   115

Test 4 Key   130

Sample answer sheets   145

Acknowledgements   150

Visual material for the Speaking test   colour section at centre of book

To the student

This book is for candidates preparing for the University of Cambridge ESOL Examinations Preliminary English Test (PET), and gives practice in all the written and oral papers. It contains four complete tests based on recent PET papers. PET tests Reading, Writing, Listening and Speaking.

PAPER 1 (1 hour and 30 minutes)

Reading

There are 35 questions in five Parts. You have to choose the right answer out of three or four options, match questions to texts or show that you think a sentence about a text is correct or incorrect.

Writing

There are three Parts: sentence transformations, a short message of 35–45 words and a letter or story of about 100 words.

PAPER 2 (about 35 minutes, including 6 minutes to transfer answers)

Listening

There are four Parts, and you will hear each of them twice. As you listen, you write your answers on the question paper. At the end, you have 6 minutes to copy your answers onto the answer sheet.

PAPER 3 (10–12 minutes for each pair of candidates)

Speaking

You take the Speaking test with another candidate. There are two examiners in the room. One examiner talks to you. This examiner sometimes asks you questions and sometimes asks you to talk to the other candidate. The other examiner listens to you. Both examiners give you marks. During the test the examiner gives you and your partner photographs and other pictures to look at and to talk about.

Preparing for PET by yourself

Reading

Have a look at some English language magazines, and read some articles about things that interest you. Look through some stories written in simplified English in your library or bookshop. Choose the ones which are interesting and just a little difficult for you, and guess the words you may not know before you look them up in your dictionary.

Writing

It can be very helpful to keep a diary in English, so that you find and learn the words that really mean something to you. You may also want to find an English-speaking pen-friend or e-pal, or to exchange letters or emails in English with a friend who is learning with you. In those letters/emails you can describe something interesting you have done, what you are doing at present or talk about your plans. In that way everything you practise will be real for you and not just an exercise.

Listening

Watch any interesting English language films at your cinema, or on TV or video whenever you can. Watch or listen to any English language teaching programmes on TV or radio. (A free list of such programmes is available from the BBC, Programme Guides, Bush House, PO Box 76, London WC2B 4PH, United Kingdom.) Listen to learning materials on cassette, so that you can hear many different kinds of voices. You may also hear people speaking English in shops, restaurants or hotels, or a tourist guide telling English-speaking visitors about places of interest in your area.

Speaking

Practise talking English with a friend who is also learning, and arrange to spend time doing this regularly. Ask each other questions, tell each other what you have enjoyed doing, talk about your daily lives, your plans, your likes and dislikes – in English. It really does get easier, once you start practising!

Further information

For more information about PET or any other Cambridge ESOL examination write to:

University of Cambridge
ESOL Examinations
1 Hills Road
Cambridge
CB1 2EU
England

Telephone: +44 1223 553355
Fax: +44 1223 460278
email: ESOLHelpdesk@ucles.org.uk
website: www.CambridgeESOL.org

In some areas this information can also be obtained from the British Council.

Test 1

PAPER 1   READING AND WRITING TEST   (1 hour 30 minutes)

READING

PART 1

Questions 1–5

- Look at the text in each question.
- What does it say?
- Mark the letter next to the correct explanation – **A**, **B** or **C** – **on your answer sheet**.

Example:

0

NO BICYCLES AGAINST GLASS PLEASE

A Do not leave your bicycle touching the window.

B Broken glass may damage your bicycle tyres.

C Your bicycle may not be safe here.

Example answer:

Part 1		
0	A ▬	B ☐ C ☐

1

UNIVERSITY LIBRARY
Please wait here
while we check
your books

A Do not go away until we have checked your books.

B Check you have all your books before you leave the library.

C Do not leave books here for checking without telling us.

2

Why has Kim emailed Sally?

A to give her some details

B to let her know that he's ill

C to remind her to do something

3

A We leave some toys at the back of this room for children.

B Please don't leave any toys outside this room when you go.

C Remember to take your children's toys with you when you leave.

4

Ed,

Dennis rang: DON'T take the main road to Madingley – there's been an accident and you won't get to the match on time. Go through Drayton instead.

Lynn

A To arrive punctually, Ed should use a different route.

B Dennis suggests that it's quicker to go on the main road.

C If there's enough time, Lynn would like to see the match.

5

Not as big a city as we expected, but that's okay. Limited nightlife, though there's plenty to see every day and travelling around is painless!

Martyna

According to Martyna, the city's disadvantage is

A its actual size.

B its transport system.

C its evening entertainment.

PART 2

Questions 6–10

- The people below are all looking for a college course.
- On the opposite page there are descriptions of eight colleges and the courses they offer.
- Decide which college (**letters A–H**) would be the most suitable for each person (**numbers 6–10**).
- For each of these numbers mark the correct letter **on your answer sheet**.

6 Anna is 18 and she wants to do computer studies so that she can work in an office. She would like to study in London but is worried about finding accommodation.

7 Peter is 19 and wants to be a sports teacher. He is very good at sport, especially running. He wants to go to a college outside London.

8 Maria used to teach in a secondary school but now wants to teach at primary level. She wants to do a part-time course in London.

9 Stephen works in the computer industry and wants to go back to college for a year to do a diploma in advanced computer studies. He lives in London and wants to study there.

10 Ali wants to do computer studies in London. He would like to do a full-time course which includes some time working in industry. In his spare time he plays football.

COURSES TO CHOOSE FROM

A **Hillman College** is a London college with up-to-date facilities. We offer both primary and secondary full-time teacher training courses. This year there will be special two-year courses available on maths and computers in the primary classroom. All students are expected to spend two terms working in local schools.

B **Kirby College** has over fifty years' experience of teacher training. We offer both full-time and part-time courses for all levels of teaching. Large college in lovely countryside, with excellent sports facilities, especially for football and athletics. There is a new course this year called 'Computers in the Classroom'.

C **Kemp College** offers a wide range of both full-time and part-time diploma courses in arts and science subjects, lasting from one to three years. The college is about two hours away from London by train. It has a new library and good student accommodation. Grants are available for students wanting to return to studying.

D **MacKintosh College** offers a range of courses from modern languages to computer studies, in a quiet and pleasant part of London. All students are offered accommodation in college flats and we have excellent sports facilities. Full-time and part-time courses of either three or four years are available.

E **Pemberley College** in central London offers full-time courses in science and computer studies. Our four-year courses allow you to spend a term every year getting work experience in different firms. There are good social and sports facilities. No college accommodation is available at present.

F **Treeholme College.** If you want to be a teacher, join one of our courses. Places are available on our full-time courses in science and maths this October. Ours is a small teacher training department in a large London college, so we can offer good facilities such as a new computer centre.

G **Dene College** was built in 1990 in an attractive part of north London. Spaces are still available on our popular part-time course in primary teaching for teachers who want to retrain. Beginning in October we will also have new four-year courses in law, economics, mathematics and sports science.

H **Westgate College** in south London has a range of courses, from maths and physics to computer studies and sports science. We offer both lower and advanced diplomas. All our courses are from one to three years in length and are particularly suitable for people with some work experience.

PART 3

Questions 11–20

- Look at the sentences below about European travel.
- Read the text on the opposite page to decide if each sentence is correct or incorrect.
- If it is correct, mark **A on your answer sheet**.
- If it is not correct, mark **B on your answer sheet**.

11 The *Daily News* is offering free flights to a number of European cities.

12 These tickets allow passengers to fly directly from Heathrow to Nice.

13 To go to Copenhagen you must leave early in the morning.

14 Travelling on Saturday costs extra.

15 The Crown Inn Hotel is convenient for shopping.

16 You must write to the newspaper for a special application form.

17 You should ring the newspaper about your reservation seven days before you are due to leave.

18 Passengers must buy insurance for the trip.

19 You must pay extra for airport tax.

20 The airline company has the right to change a flight without telling passengers in advance.

TAKE THIS GREAT OPPORTUNITY TO DISCOVER SOME WONDERFUL EUROPEAN CITIES

Here is a wonderful flight offer from the *Daily News*, giving our readers the chance to get a return ticket to Europe for next to nothing.

European destinations

Our basic offer price of £10 allows you to take an Express Airlines flight to Brussels in Belgium from Heathrow Airport in London. At Brussels Airport there are connections to Nice, Milan, Madrid or Copenhagen for only an extra £25 return.

This offer is available from November to February, apart from the period December 18 – January 6. There are up to five flights during the day between Heathrow and Brussels. If you plan to travel further than Brussels, you will need to get the early morning flight from Heathrow. A charge of £10 is added to the ticket price for travel between Friday and Sunday.

So much to see and do

Why not treat yourself and your partner or friend to a few days in Belgium? Discover wonderful Brussels, which is much more than the centre of the European Union. The Belgian capital is a mix of old and new, with a historic central square, a number of galleries and museums to explore, and more restaurants per person than any other city in Europe. The *Daily News* is also organising tours of the beautiful Belgian towns of Bruges and Antwerp. There is also the opportunity for our readers to stay at the Crown Inn Hotel in Brussels and enjoy luxury accommodation and friendly service for an amazing price starting from £15 per person per night. The Crown Inn Hotel is in a perfect position for you to see the sights and look round the city shops. Or you can simply relax in this friendly hotel, which offers leisure facilities and family rooms, making it a great place for people with children.

How to get your tickets

We will only consider bookings made on the special application form printed in our newspaper, and sent to us with a cheque for the fare. One week before departure, please contact our office by phone to check your booking.

We recommend that you get travel insurance for your trip. Please note that the prices do not include airport tax. Once bookings are made, no changes are allowed, and your money cannot be returned if you cancel. Any flight may be changed or cancelled by the airline company without notice.

PART 4

Questions 21–25

- Read the text and questions below.
- For each question, mark the letter next to the correct answer – **A**, **B**, **C** or **D** – **on your answer sheet.**

John Fisher, a builder, and his wife Elizabeth wanted more living space, so they left their small flat for an old 40-metre-high castle tower. They have spent five years turning it into a beautiful home with six floors, winning three architectural prizes.

'I love the space, and being private,' Elizabeth says. 'You feel separated from the world. If I'm in the kitchen, which is 25 metres above the ground floor, and the doorbell rings, I don't have to answer it because visitors can't see I'm in!'

'There are 142 steps to the top, so if I go up and down five or six times a day, it's very good exercise! But having to carry heavy things to the top is terrible, so I never buy more than two bags of shopping from the supermarket at a time. Apart from that, it's a brilliant place to live.'

'When we first saw the place, I asked my father's advice about buying it, because we couldn't decide. After paying for it, we were a bit worried because it looked awful. But we really loved it, and knew how we wanted it to look.'

'Living here can be difficult – yesterday I climbed a four-metre ladder to clean the windows. But when you stand on the roof you can see all the way out to sea on a clear day, and that's a wonderful experience. I'm really glad we moved.'

---

21   What is the writer trying to do in the text?

    A   describe how to turn an old tower into a house
    B   recommend a particular builder
    C   describe what it is like to live in a tower
    D   explain how to win prizes for building work

22   From this text, a reader can find out

    A   why visitors are not welcome at John and Elizabeth's house.
    B   why Elizabeth exercises every day.
    C   why Elizabeth asked her father to buy the tower.
    D   why John and Elizabeth left their flat.

23 Which of the following best describes Elizabeth's feelings about the tower?

  A   She wanted it as soon as she saw it.
  B   She likes most things about it.
  C   She has been worried since they paid for it.
  D   She finds it unsuitable to live in.

24 What problem does Elizabeth have with living in such a tall building?

  A   Her visitors find it difficult to see if she is at home.
  B   She feels separated from other people.
  C   She cannot bring home lots of shopping at once.
  D   It is impossible to clean any of the windows.

25 How will John and Elizabeth advertise their tower if they sell it?

A

> **FOR SALE**
> **Tall building, formerly a castle. High windows give a good view. Needs some improvement.**

B

> FOR SALE
> A house with a difference – a castle tower, turned into a lovely home.
> Wonderful view.

C

> **FOR SALE**
> Prize-winning home, five years old. Six rooms, all with sea views.

D

> **FOR SALE**
> **Castle tower, turned into six small flats, close to supermarket.**

PART 5

Questions 26–35

- Read the text below and choose the correct word for each space.
- For each question, mark the letter next to the correct word – **A**, **B**, **C** or **D** – on **your answer sheet**.

Example answer:

	Part 5
0	A ■ B ▭ C ▭ D ▭

CAMPING

Although **(0)** .... groups of people have always lived outdoors in tents, camping as we know it today only began to be **(26)** .... about 50 years ago. The increase in the use of cars and improvements in camping **(27)** .... have allowed more people to travel longer **(28)** .... into the countryside and to stay there in greater comfort.

Many campers like to be **(29)** .... themselves in quiet areas, so they **(30)** .... their tent and food and walk or cycle into the forests or the mountains. Others, preferring to be near people, drive to a public or privately-owned campsite **(31)** .... has up-to-date facilities, **(32)** .... hot showers and swimming pools.

Whether campers are **(33)** .... in the mountains or on a busy site, they should remember to **(34)** .... the area clean and tidy. In the forests, they must put out any fires and keep food hidden to avoid attracting **(35)** .... animals.

0	**A** some	**B** every	**C** both	**D** each
26	**A** famous	**B** popular	**C** favourite	**D** current
27	**A** tools	**B** baggage	**C** equipment	**D** property
28	**A** ways	**B** directions	**C** voyages	**D** distances
29	**A** on	**B** by ✓	**C** at	**D** of
30	**A** take	**B** make	**C** pick	**D** do
31	**A** where	**B** who	**C** which	**D** when
32	**A** such	**B** like	**C** as	**D** just
33	**A** lonely	**B** single	**C** separate	**D** alone
34	**A** remain	**B** stay	**C** leave	**D** let
35	**A** wild	**B** natural	**C** loose	**D** free

WRITING

PART 1

Questions 1–5

- Here are some sentences about a student who is living in a flat.
- For each question, complete the second sentence so that it means the same as the first, **using no more than three words.**
- **Write only the missing words on your answer sheet.**

> **Example:**   The flat is near my college.
>
> **The flat is not** .far from.. **my college.**

1   My friend told me that I could stay in his flat.

    My friend said: 'You .... **my flat.'**

2   I started living here two months ago.

    I have lived here .... **two months ago.**

3   This is the first time I've lived in a city.

    I've .... **in a city before.**

4   The flat has two bedrooms.

    There .... **in the flat.**

5   My bedroom is too small for all my books.

    My bedroom is not .... **for all my books.**

PART 2

Question 6

You have just joined a club in your area and you think your English friend Max would enjoy going there with you.

Write an email to Max. In your email, you should

- **explain which club you have joined**
- **suggest Max should visit the club**
- **say what you could do there together.**

Write 35–45 words on your answer sheet.

PART 3

Answer **one** of the following questions (**7** or **8**).

Question 7

- This is part of a letter you receive from a friend in the U.S.A.

 I guess there are many traditional festivals in your country. What's the most important one? Why do people celebrate this festival? Write and tell me all about it!

- Now write a letter, answering your friend's questions.
- Write your **letter** in about 100 words **on your answer sheet**.

Question 8

- Your English teacher has asked you to write a story.
- Your story must begin with this sentence:

Nobody knew what Adam had in his suitcase.

- Write your **story** in about 100 words **on your answer sheet**.

PAPER 2   LISTENING TEST   about 35 minutes
(including 6 minutes transfer time)

PART 1

Questions 1–7

- There are seven questions in this part.
- For each question there are three pictures and a short recording.
- Choose the correct picture and put a tick (✓) in the box below it.

Example: Where did the man leave his camera?

A ✓   B ☐   C ☐

1   Which activity will the family do this year?

A ☐   B ☐   C ☐

2   Which is the woman's house?

A ☐   B ☐   C ☐

3 Why will drivers have problems this morning?

A ☐

B ☐

C ☐

4 What time will Robin leave the house?

A ☐

B ☐

C ☐

5 What did Simon do this morning?

A ☐

B ☐

C ☐

6   What hasn't the girl packed yet?

A ☐   B ☐   C ☐

7   What has the woman just bought?

A   B ☐   C ☐

PART 2

Questions 8–13

- You will hear an interview with Angela Morgan, who has recently flown around the world in a helicopter.
- For each question, put a tick (✓) in the correct box.

8 The main reason for Angela's trip was to

A ☐ make money for her business.

B ☐ make money for other people.

C ☐ have an exciting adventure.

9 What does Angela say about her life now?

A ☐ She feels much older.

B ☐ She likes to be active and busy.

C ☐ She is lonely without her children.

10 When Angela had flying lessons

A ☐ her course lasted five months.

B ☐ her husband took lessons as well.

C ☐ she got to know her teacher well.

11 During the trip, Angela and her teacher

A ☐ did very little sightseeing.

B ☐ carried all the water they needed.

C ☐ had engine problems several times.

12 What did Angela enjoy most about the trip?

A ☐ flying at night

B ☐ walking in the desert

C ☐ watching the changes in the scenery

13 What did Angela miss most while she was away?

A ☐ modern bathrooms

B ☐ regular exercise

C ☐ interesting entertainment

PART 3

Questions 14–19

- You will hear a radio announcer talking about activities at a museum called Science World.
- For each question, fill in the missing information in the numbered space.

Science World

Next week's Special Events

EVENTS: TIME OF DAY:

* Electricity workshop   **(14)** ....
* Experiments with water   *Wednesday morning*

* Talk about space travel by   *Saturday evening*
  well-known scientist from
  (15) ....

Science World entrance fees are: £3.00 Adults
                                   £2.00 Children

Tickets for Special Events cost extra: **(16)** £ .... Adults

                                        Reduced prices for children

Get tickets direct from Science World on 284311,

                          or from the **(17)** ....

Newton Café is next to the **(18)** ....
(snacks available all day).

Phone Science World for free ticket to exhibition about

(19) ....

PART 4

Questions 20–25

- Look at the six sentences for this part.
- You will hear a conversation between a boy, Tom, and his sister, Clare, about school.
- Decide if each sentence is correct or incorrect.
- If it is correct, put a tick (✓) in the box under **A** for **YES**. If it is not correct, put a tick (✓) in the box under **B** for **NO**.

		A YES	B NO
20	Clare thinks their father will be pleased by Tom's news.	☐	☐
21	Tom believes he can manage both swimming and school work.	☐	☐
22	Tom's teacher thinks Tom is clever.	☐	☐
23	Tom dislikes doing maths.	☐	☐
24	Clare thinks it is a bad idea to take a friend's advice.	☐	☐
25	Tom finally realises he will need his father's agreement to his plans.	☐	☐

About the Speaking test

The Speaking test lasts about 10 to 12 minutes. You take the test with another candidate. There are two examiners in the room. One examiner talks to you and the other examiner listens to you. Both the examiners give you marks.

Part 1

The examiners introduce themselves and then one examiner asks you and your partner to say your names and spell them. This examiner then asks you questions about yourself, your daily life, interests, etc.

Part 2

The examiner asks you to talk about something together and gives you a drawing to help you.

Part 3

You each have a chance to talk by yourselves. The examiner gives you a colour photograph to look at and asks you to talk about it. When you have finished talking, the examiner gives your partner a different photograph to look at and to talk about.

Part 4

The examiner asks you and your partner to say more about the subject of the photographs in Part 3. You may be asked to give your opinion or to talk about something that has happened to you.

Test 2

PAPER 1 READING AND WRITING TEST (1 hour 30 minutes)

READING

PART 1

Questions 1–5

- Look at the text in each question.
- What does it say?
- Mark the letter next to the correct explanation – **A**, **B** or **C** – **on your answer sheet**.

Example:

0

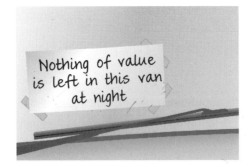

A Valuable objects are removed at night.

B Valuables should not be left in the van.

C This van is locked at night.

Example answer:

Part 1		
0	A ▬	B ☐	C ☐

1

A Lock your cycle near this gate before entering.

B Cyclists should use a different entrance when this one is locked.

C If the side gate is locked, go through the cycle entrance.

2

> **£25**
> **RESERVES ANY**
> **PICTURE**
> **IN THE GALLERY**

A We will keep any picture for you if you give us £25.

B Some of the pictures in the gallery are reserved.

C It costs £25 to show your picture in the gallery.

3

> It's raining in Manchester, so am visiting museums. Here for the day with Ellen, who's at a college interview right now. Driving home together tonight.
>
> Love Annette

A Ellen and Annette are spending the day together sightseeing.

B Annette is writing this card while Ellen attends an interview.

C Ellen is staying overnight in Manchester, but Annette isn't.

4

> **SPORTS HALL**
> **Final five minutes of bookings must be used to put equipment away** .

A Bookings now include an extra five minutes for equipment to be put away.

B You have five minutes after bookings have finished to return any sports equipment used.

C The hall must be cleared of equipment in the five minutes before bookings end.

5

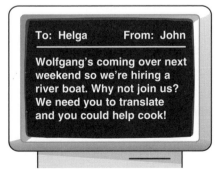

> To: Helga　　From: John
>
> Wolfgang's coming over next weekend so we're hiring a river boat. Why not join us? We need you to translate and you could help cook!

John wants Helga to

A find a boat for hire on the river.

B do all the cooking on the holiday.

C help those on board to communicate.

PART 2

Questions 6–10

- The people below all want to move to a new home.
- On the opposite page there are descriptions of eight different homes.
- Decide which home (**letters A–H**) would be the most suitable for each of the following people (**numbers 6–10**).
- For each of these numbers mark the correct letter **on your answer sheet**.

6 Chris and Sarah want to rent a flat as soon as possible. They would prefer a quiet part of town with views over gardens and water.

7 George would like to rent a small home near the centre of town with somewhere safe to keep his car. He has only a little time to do the gardening.

8 Graham and Suzie have four children. They want to buy a house in the countryside which is big enough for each child to have their own room. The children enjoy playing outdoors.

9 Mary is a lawyer who works mainly in London. She is hoping to buy a home in the country where she can work sometimes. She needs to be able to catch a train to London easily.

10 James and Miranda have always lived in town, but as their two teenage daughters love riding they now want to buy a house in the country. They need enough space to have two horses.

Looking for a new home?

A Tidmarsh

This six-bedroom, nineteenth-century house, just outside the village of Tidmarsh, is a very pleasant family home with two sitting rooms and a dining room. There is a garage and a garden with a swimming pool. Quick sale wanted.

B Brettisham

This elegant one-bedroom house near the river consists of an unusually large living room, bright kitchen and bathroom. It has gas central heating, a small garden which is easy to look after, and a garage. Reasonable monthly rent for a town centre property.

C Lower Farleigh

For sale: this newly-built one-bedroom town house has a large lounge, kitchen, bathroom, garage and a private garden at the back that needs some work. It is very close to the shopping centre and within five minutes' walk of the bus station with connections to London and Birmingham.

D Corbridge

A lovely, furnished apartment away from the noise of the city centre, with a balcony looking down on beautiful lawns, flowers and, beyond them, the River Thames. The accommodation includes two bedrooms, a living room and a kitchen/dining room. Cars may be parked in the road. Available to rent immediately.

E Dinton

A beautiful small cottage for sale in a pretty village with lovely views over farms and hills. The accommodation includes two bedrooms, kitchen, living room and study/office. Enjoy the quiet of the countryside and still benefit from good connections with all major cities as the railway station is very close.

F Winchcombe

For sale: an interesting old country farmhouse with two reception rooms, comfortable kitchen and three bedrooms. Next to the house there are some old buildings which could be used to store equipment or keep animals, and a field which could be turned into a garden with tennis court or swimming pool.

G Saxford

A spacious new two-bedroom apartment will become available for rent when the owner moves abroad in three months' time. It has views of the park and canal although it is only one street away from the main shopping area. No private parking facilities are included but there is usually space to park in the street outside.

H Beckington

For immediate rent: an attractive, large nineteenth-century town house with ten bedrooms. At the end of the garden, there is an old building, originally used for horses, which could be used as a garage or turned into office accommodation.

PART 3

Questions 11–20

- Look at the sentences below about the island of Petulia.
- Read the text on the opposite page to decide if each sentence is correct or incorrect.
- If it is correct, mark **A on your answer sheet**.
- If it is not correct, mark **B on your answer sheet**.

11   People have lived on the island for more than 400 years.

12   There is a big difference between day-time and night-time temperatures on
      the island.

13   The islanders have sold their salt to other countries since the 1970s.

14   It takes three hours to reach Petulia from the nearest port.

15   Some farmers have more pieces of land to look after than others.

16   The animals are moved onto different land every year.

17   Boys often play football on the school field.

18   Both adults and children help to make the islanders' clothes.

19   It is likely that there will be a tourist hotel on the island soon.

20   Tourists pay to stay with families.

THE ISLAND OF PETULIA

Geography

Petulia Island is only 5.5 kilometres long and 1.5 kilometres at its widest point. It lies in the middle of Lake Donika, and is 3,900 metres above sea level. Petulia has had a small number of underlined inhabitants for over four centuries. It now has a population of 1,500 people. It has no roads, no cars or bicycles, and no electricity. The sun is extremely hot during the day but temperatures at night regularly fall well below freezing. The water of Lake Donika is 10 degrees Celsius all year round.

The past

Until recently, the island was separate from the outside world. Before the introduction of motorboats in the 1970s, travelling from Petulia to the nearest port could take over 20 hours. This journey was therefore made only once a year in order to buy salt. Motorboats have now cut the journey time to three hours, bringing new trade and tourists to Petulia.

Farming

Petulia is divided into six farming areas. Each farmer owns one piece of land in each of the six areas and grows vegetables, potatoes and cereal. Every year, farmers leave a different piece of land unplanted to allow the earth to rest. Cows and sheep are kept here during this time to improve the soil. The food grown by each farmer is shared by everyone: none is for sale. Petulia's farming year is divided into wet and dry seasons. The wet season is the busiest time. All land is dug by hand, using spades. In the dry season between July and August, the islanders have time to build new houses, repair stone walls and make clothes. Men knit traditional clothes from wool that is prepared by the women.

Education

Petulia has a well-equipped primary and secondary school. There is a good-sized sports field, but instead of playing football the boys usually choose to knit, like their fathers, while the girls make wool. Walking along the rough tracks of the island, tourists often see small children on their way to and from school.

Visitors

Petulia has a tourist industry but the people have kept their traditional customs. They recently voted against a hotel development plan, so there will be no hotels on the island. Instead, tourists are placed with a family as guests. The money earned by each family is, like all money on the island, equally divided. During the dry season, many islanders entertain tourists late into the cold nights with pipe music and dances.

PART 4

Questions 21–25

- Read the text and questions below.
- For each question, mark the letter next to the correct answer – **A**, **B**, **C** or **D** – **on your answer sheet.**

The shoemaker

Bill Bird is a shoemaker who cannot make shoes fast enough for his growing number of customers – and he charges more than £300 for a pair! Customers travel hundreds of kilometres to his London shoe clinic or to his workshop in the countryside to have their feet measured. He makes shoes for people with feet of unusual sizes: very large, very small, very broad or very narrow. The shoes are at least as fashionable as those found in ordinary shops.

Mr Bird says: 'My problem is that I cannot find skilled workers. Young people all seem to prefer to work with computers these days. We will lose the necessary skills soon because there are fewer and fewer shoemakers nowadays. I am 45, and now I want to teach young people everything I know about making shoes. It's a good job, and a lot of people want to buy beautiful shoes specially made for them.'

He started in the business 19 years ago and now he employs three other people. His customers pay about £500 for their first pair of shoes. He says: 'Our customers come because they want comfortable shoes which are exactly the right size.' Extra pairs of shoes cost between £320 and £450, as it takes one employee a whole week to make just one shoe.

---

21 What is the writer trying to do in the text?

    A   describe where Mr Bird finds his staff
    B   encourage people to wear comfortable shoes
    C   advertise a job selling expensive shoes
    D   show Mr Bird's worries about his trade

22 What can readers find out from this text?

    A   how many customers Mr Bird has
    B   how to make shoes like Mr Bird
    C   how to get to Mr Bird's London shop
    D   how much Mr Bird's shoes cost

23 What is Mr Bird's opinion of young people?

    A   They want too much money.
    B   They are difficult to train.
    C   They prefer other jobs.
    D   They don't work hard enough.

24 Customers choose Mr Bird because his shoes

    A   are the most fashionable.
    B   fit perfectly.
    C   look very unusual.
    D   are traditional in design.

25 Which advertisement would Mr Bird put in a newspaper?

A

> **Wanted – experienced shoemakers to work in large shoe company in London. Good rates of pay.**

B

> **Wanted – young people to train as shoemakers. Must be able to use a computer.**

C

> **Wanted – young people to train as shoemakers. Good job with small company.**

D

> **Wanted – country workshop needs people for unskilled jobs working with shoes.**

PART 5

Questions 26–35

- Read the text below and choose the correct word for each space.
- For each question, mark the letter next to the correct word – **A**, **B**, **C** or **D** – **on your answer sheet**.

Example answer:

	Part 5
0	A ■ B ▭ C ▭ D ▭

THE ESCALATOR

An American, Charles D. Seeberger, invented moving stairs to transport people **(0)** .... the 1890s. He **(26)** .... this invention an 'escalator', **(27)** .... the name from the Latin word 'scala', **(28)** .... means 'ladder'. Escalators move people up and down short **(29)** .... Lifts do the same, but only move **(30)** .... small number of people. If an escalator breaks down, it can still be **(31)** .... as ordinary stairs. An escalator can move **(32)** .... 8,000 and 9,600 people an hour, and it **(33)** .... not need a person to operate it.

Towards the end of the nineteenth century, cities were **(34)** .... more crowded and the first escalators were built at railway stations and in big department **(35)** .... , so that people could move about more quickly. Today we see escalators everywhere.

0	**A** in	**B** at	**C** by	**D** on
26	**A** announced	**B** called	**C** translated	**D** explained
27	**A** fetching	**B** lending	**C** taking	**D** carrying
28	**A** what	**B** whose	**C** who	**D** which
29	**A** distances	**B** directions	**C** measurements	**D** lengths
30	**A** the	**B** a	**C** some	**D** any
31	**A** walked	**B** made	**C** used	**D** changed
32	**A** from	**B** between	**C** to	**D** above
33	**A** is	**B** has	**C** did	**D** does
34	**A** coming	**B** becoming	**C** continuing	**D** developing
35	**A** stores	**B** shops	**C** places	**D** houses

WRITING

PART 1

Questions 1–5

- Here are some sentences about daily travel.
- For each question, complete the second sentence so that it means the same as the first, **using no more than three words**.
- **Write only the missing words on your answer sheet**.

> **Example:** Going by bus is quicker than cycling.
>
> **Cycling** .takes longer than. **going by bus.**

1 Maria lives a long way from her office.

Maria's office isn't .... **her home.**

2 It is a forty-minute bus journey to her office.

The bus journey to her office .... **forty minutes.**

3 Driving a car in the town centre is not allowed.

You are not allowed .... **cars in the town centre.**

4 Maria sometimes takes a taxi although it is expensive.

Maria doesn't often take a taxi .... **it is expensive.**

5 Yesterday she got up too late to catch the bus.

Yesterday she got up so late that she .... **the bus.**

PART 2

Question 6

You are planning a surprise party for your cousin and want to invite an English-speaking friend to the party.

Write a card to send to your friend. In your card, you should

- **invite your friend to the party**
- **say when it will take place**
- **explain why you want to surprise your cousin.**

Write 35–45 words on your answer sheet.

PART 3

Answer **one** of the following questions (**7** or **8**).

Question 7

- This is part of a letter you receive from your pen-friend.

> I've just bought a new computer game. Do you like playing games on the computer – or have you got a Play Station? What else do you use the computer for?

- Now write a letter, answering your pen-friend's questions.
- Write your **letter** in about 100 words **on your answer sheet**.

Question 8

- You have to write a story for your English teacher.
- Your story must have this title:

Winning the prize

- Write your **story** in about 100 words **on your answer sheet**.

PAPER 2   LISTENING TEST   about 35 minutes
(including 6 minutes transfer time)

PART 1

Questions 1–7

- There are seven questions in this part.
- For each question there are three pictures and a short recording.
- Choose the correct picture and put a tick (✓) in the box below it.

Example: What's the time?

A ✓   B ☐   C ☐

1   How much is the man's ticket?

A ☐   B ☐   C ☐

2   What will they have for lunch?

A ☐   B ☐   C ☐

3 Why was the man late home?

A ☐

B ☐

C ☐

4 What was the weather like on John's holiday?

A ☐

B ☐

C ☐

5 What time was the woman's appointment?

A ☐

B ☐

C ☐

6 What did the woman buy?

 A ☐

 B ☐

 C ☐

7 Where are the man and the woman talking?

 A ☐

 B ☐

 C ☐

PART 2

Questions 8–13

- You will hear a woman called Sarah talking to a group of people about her painting.
- For each question put a tick (✓) in the correct box.

8 How often does Sarah paint now?

    A ☐ three days a week

    B ☐ five days a week

    C ☐ every evening

9 Sarah earns enough money from her painting to

    A ☐ give up her computing job.

    B ☐ pay for her flat and car.

    C ☐ pay for her artist's materials.

10 When she was at primary school, Sarah

    A ☐ painted pictures of people.

    B ☐ learnt to use chalk.

    C ☐ drew scenes in pencil.

11 What pleased Sarah most about her painting holidays?

    A ☐ meeting other artists

    B ☐ seeing beautiful scenery

    C ☐ receiving individual teaching

12 Which of these has Sarah done?

A ☐ painted people in Greece

B ☐ painted sunrises in Scotland

C ☐ watched birds in Spain

13 After watching Sarah's video, the audience will

A ☐ fill in a questionnaire about the talk.

B ☐ look round an art exhibition.

C ☐ have a break and a drink.

PART 3

Questions 14–19

- You will hear a radio programme giving you information about the city of Glasgow.
- For each question, fill in the missing information in the numbered space.

GLASGOW

Arrival by car

* City centre car parks are **(14)** .... Leave car at hotel.

'Discovering Glasgow' tour bus

* Departs from George **(15)** .... every 30 minutes.

* Buy tickets from **(16)** ....

Walking

* Go to Welcome Centre for information – free **(17)** .... available.

Places to visit

* Glasgow Cathedral – built in fifteenth century.

* Merchant City area – shops selling **(18)** .... and clothes.

* Byres Road – student area.

* Botanic Gardens – glasshouses close at **(19)** ....

PART 4

Questions 20–25

- Look at the six sentences for this part.
- You will hear a conversation between a boy, Frank, and a girl, Linda, in a music shop.
- Decide if each sentence is correct or incorrect.
- If it is correct, put a tick (✓) in the box under **A** for **YES**. If it is not correct, put a tick (✓) in the box under **B** for **NO**.

		A YES	B NO
20	Linda wants to change a cassette because she dislikes it.	☐	☐
21	Linda already knows what she wants to get.	☐	☐
22	Frank recommends a famous band.	☐	☐
23	Linda is happy with her cassette player.	☐	☐
24	Linda thinks the price of the cassette is reasonable.	☐	☐
25	Linda has already seen the Irish band.	☐	☐

About the Speaking test

The Speaking test lasts about 10 to 12 minutes. You take the test with another candidate. There are two examiners in the room. One examiner talks to you and the other examiner listens to you. Both the examiners give you marks.

Part 1

The examiners introduce themselves and then one examiner asks you and your partner to say your names and spell them. This examiner then asks you questions about yourself, your daily life, interests, etc.

Part 2

The examiner asks you to talk about something together and gives you a drawing to help you.

Part 3

You each have a chance to talk by yourselves. The examiner gives you a colour photograph to look at and asks you to talk about it. When you have finished talking, the examiner gives your partner a different photograph to look at and to talk about.

Part 4

The examiner asks you and your partner to say more about the subject of the photographs in Part 3. You may be asked to give your opinion or to talk about something that has happened to you.

Test 3

PAPER 1   READING AND WRITING TEST   (1 hour 30 minutes)

READING

PART 1

Questions 1–5

- Look at the text in each question.
- What does it say?
- Mark the letter next to the correct explanation – **A**, **B** or **C** – **on your answer sheet**.

Example:

0

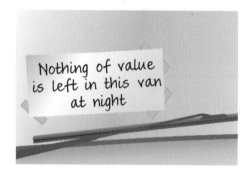

A Valuable objects are removed at night.

B Valuables should not be left in the van.

C This van is locked at night.

Example answer:

	Part 1		
0	<u>A</u>	B	C

1

> Phil
> Gary's phoned twice about the team list for Friday's match. Could you email it to him as soon as you get in?
>
> See you later,
> Beth

What must Phil do on his return?

A phone Gary about the team list for Friday's match

B get Gary to play in the football match on Friday

C let Gary know who's playing football on Friday

2

> Keiko,
> It was nice to see you yesterday.
> I forgot to ask about your new
> job. Well done! You must be
> pleased. Let's meet for lunch
> soon.
> *Jane*

What is Jane doing in this card?

A thanking Keiko for lunch

B offering Keiko congratulations

C giving Keiko some information

3

STUDENT CANTEEN

**Please show your meal
ticket or you must pay
the full amount**

A Students can buy meal tickets here at a discount.

B Students are charged the normal price if they forget their meal tickets.

C Students can buy food up to the amount shown on their meal tickets.

4

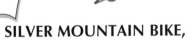

SILVER MOUNTAIN BIKE,
IN GOOD CONDITION AND NOT
EVEN TWO YEARS OLD!
QUICK SALE NEEDED.
OFFERS WELCOME (NOT LESS
THAN £80 PLEASE)
RICK 0798 453 668

A Rick would accept £80 for his bike.

B Rick's bike only needs a few repairs.

C Rick bought his bike two years ago.

5

**NO TURNING BY
VEHICLES AT ANY TIME**
Factory entrance
always in use

A Do not use this entrance to return vehicles to the factory.

B Factory vehicles are turning here all the time.

C Do not turn here as this entrance is used all the time.

PART 2

Questions 6–10

- The people below all want to visit an interesting city.
- On the opposite page there are descriptions of eight cities.
- Decide which city (**letters A–H**) would be the most suitable for each of the following people (**numbers 6–10**).
- For each of these numbers mark the correct letter **on your answer sheet**.

6

Ryana has just finished her business degree. She would like to relax in a clean, quiet city which has a long history.

7

Kevin has just finished his economics degree. He would like to visit a city that has a big business centre and also offers traditional goods for the tourist to buy.

8

Mandy and her seventy-year-old aunt share an interest in painting and buying valuable, old objects. They would like to go to a city where they can shop easily and look at art.

9

Dhillon is studying international business. He would like to go to a city where the inhabitants come from many different countries, which will give him the opportunity to try a variety of food.

10

Jenny and Mavis want to escape from modern life and go somewhere more traditional. They would like to go on some long trips outside the city as well.

Cities to Visit

A Kadia

This busy city has developed beside the main river which divides the central commercial district into two parts. Although you will find the main offices of many international companies, you can still ride on a water taxi and visit the side streets which sell colourful locally-made clothes and crafts.

B Drummore

This is one of the world's cleanest and most modern cities. There are lots of top-class hotels offering a range of international dishes. It is sunny all year round. Traffic is not a problem on the roads in and around the city, but travel is limited outside the main city area as it is mainly desert.

C Noien

This is a cultural centre with 33 museums and galleries, many attached to colleges and universities. It is not a historical city but it contains some interesting buildings, including the Post Office, which has a silver roof. It has noisy markets selling everything from antiques to plants.

D Polatika

The streets of this city are full both day and night. It is built on a river and the best way to see it is on a tourist boat which passes the beautiful old buildings. The city is starting to grow and has just opened its first department stores.

E Haristor

This famous city has been on the same site for over a thousand years. Old and new exist together and there isn't the fast pace of most cities. The streets are wide and well-kept with plenty of trees. Search carefully and you will find some outdoor markets and food stalls in this peaceful environment.

F Lotten

This is a regional centre for trade and tourism and is completely 'up-to-date'. People who live in this city come from many different parts of the world and so there is an excellent choice of restaurants. There is a wonderful transport system, and modern department stores.

G Foforon

There are plenty of tours to take from the city and visitors can go to mountains, farms and villages. This small city has changed little over time and its streets and markets are still crowded and noisy.

H Quinter

There is a lot of modern painting and sculpture in this relatively new city where many nationalities have come together. The galleries are well hidden though, and not easy to get to by public transport. This is mainly used for getting people in and out of the business centre, where there are many office blocks.

PART 3

Questions 11–20

- Look at the sentences below about Highfield House.
- Read the text on the opposite page to decide if each sentence is correct or incorrect.
- If it is correct, mark **A on your answer sheet**.
- If it is not correct, mark **B on your answer sheet**.

11   Highfield House is near the seaside.

12   The current inhabitants belong to the Highfield family.

13   Things which used to be used in the House are part of the exhibition.

14   It is sometimes possible to have a boat ride.

15   Highfield House has an exhibition of old farming equipment.

16   The shop sells paintings by artists who work in the area.

17   You can buy plants in what was formerly the walled garden.

18   The tea room can supply picnics.

19   The House is closed on Sundays in July.

20   If you have between 10 and 20 people in your group, cheaper tickets are available.

Highfield House

Come and enjoy three hundred years of history in a single day! Highfield House is one of Britain's finest old buildings, with attractive, well-kept gardens and good views of the beautiful North Norfolk coast.

Until recently, it was the home of members of the Highfield family. Now, however, this classic 18th-century hall is a living museum full of art and history, where many objects belonging to its past inhabitants can be seen and enjoyed by the public.

Highfield House really does have something for everyone. There are so many attractions, from the beautiful state rooms to the peaceful picnic places by the lake. You can even have a trip on the water if the weather is suitable.

Enjoy a guided tour of the House, starting with the grandeur of the entrance, and carry on through the various rooms. (Visitors should note that some rooms may be closed for repairs.) The tour of the House ends in the old kitchen.

Highfield also has a large collection of objects which were once used on the farm, such as early planting and harvesting machines and steam engines. These can be seen in a separate building near the House.

You will also find many wonderful examples of the work of local painters for sale in the shop. And don't miss the beautiful Garden Centre on the site of what used to be the old 18th-century walled garden. The Centre has a good range of trees, shrubs and plants for sale and is open the whole year. (See below for House opening times.)

Visit the gift shop for really useful presents for all the family, and have a look in the art gallery at the collection of beautiful pictures belonging to the owners of Highfield House. Follow your visit with a delicious afternoon tea in the comfort of the tea room. Or, if you don't wish to be inside, why not bring your own picnic with you to have in the park, before walking beside the lake to see the many different kinds of birds there? What is more, in the summer, the clean sandy beaches make a perfect place for children to play.

HOUSE OPENING TIMES:
Daily 2.00 p.m. to 5.00 p.m. from the beginning of June to the end of September (except Sundays and Mondays – 11.30 a.m. to 5.00 p.m.)

Last admission on any day 4.40 p.m.

ADMISSION:
Adults £5   Children £2.50
10% discount on tickets if over 20 people.

PARKING:
Plenty of free parking for cars. Good facilities for coaches.

PART 4

Questions 21–25

- Read the text and questions below.
- For each question, mark the letter next to the correct answer – **A**, **B**, **C** or **D** –
  on your answer sheet.

If you want to take the whole family on holiday, and keep everybody happy, then I have found just the place for you. I recently went with a group of friends to stay at the Greenwood Holiday Village, which is open from May until October.

Built in the centre of a forest, Greenwood is a great place to stay whatever the weather. Its main attraction for families is the indoor World of Water, where young and old can have fun in the different pools. Some of these, however, are for serious swimmers only.

For sporty people, the Country Club offers tennis, squash and badminton. If your children are too young to join in these sports, there are activity clubs. Greenwood is a good place for families as it is traffic-free – you explore on foot or by bike. Some people complained that this was inconvenient, but I was pleased to be out in the fresh air. For evening entertainment, there are shows and cinemas.

Accommodation is in a variety of apartments of different sizes. These have up to four bedrooms, a kitchen and a bathroom, as well as a dining area. Before going, I thought the apartments might not be big enough for all of us, but I was pleasantly surprised – it was not too crowded at all.

I'll definitely go back to Greenwood next year. Why don't you give it a try? Visit their website for further information now!

---

21 What is the writer's main purpose in writing this text?

    A   to give her opinion of the holiday village

    B   to describe what her family did at the holiday village

    C   to give advice to a friend going to the holiday village

    D   to complain about the holiday village

22 From the text, the reader can find out

    A   the best way to get to the holiday village.

    B   the best time of year to visit the holiday village.

    C   what activities are available at the holiday village.

    D   how to reserve accommodation at the holiday village.

23 What does the writer think about the holiday village?

    A The apartments there are not big enough.
    B It is not convenient because you cannot use your car.
    C It can only be enjoyed in good weather.
    D There is something there for all ages.

24 What does the writer say about the apartments?

    A There is not much space between them.
    B Each one has its own bathroom.
    C They all have four bedrooms.
    D Not all of them have dining areas.

25 Which postcard would somebody send from the holiday village?

A

> Dear Jane,
> The children love the beach and all the activities. We've got a lovely 4-bedroom apartment.
>
> Love,
> Ann

B

> Dear Jane,
> As it's April, the weather isn't good, but it doesn't matter as there's a lovely swimming pool.
>
> Love,
> Ann

C

> Dear Jane,
> My parents love the swimming pool, and the children love riding around the forest on their bicycles.
>
> Love,
> Ann

D

> Dear Jane,
> We're a bit disappointed that we have to drive everywhere, but there's lots to see and do.
>
> Love,
> Ann

PART 5

Questions 26–35

- Read the text below and choose the correct word for each space.
- For each question, mark the letter next to the correct word – **A**, **B**, **C** or **D** – **on your answer sheet**.

Example answer:

	Part 5
0	A ■ B ▢ C ▢ D ▢

WILLIAM THE HERO!

Brave William Baldock, **(0)** .... is six years old, is a hero after helping his mother when she fell downstairs. William quickly rang **(26)** .... an ambulance when he discovered his mother had broken her leg. In spite of being frightened, he **(27)** .... the emergency services what had happened and answered all the questions they asked him. He also telephoned his father **(28)** .... work, and then his grandmother, to explain what he had **(29)** .... While waiting for **(30)** .... people to come, William looked after his 18-month-old sister.

When ambulance man Steve Lyn went to the house, he was amazed: 'It's **(31)** .... that a young boy of six knew the right number to **(32)** .... , and was able to give us the correct information. **(33)** .... of William's quick thinking, we were able to **(34)** .... there immediately.'

Mrs Baldock left hospital yesterday, very **(35)** .... to both William and the ambulance service.

0	**A** who	**B** that	**C** which	**D** whose
26	**A** to	**B** off	**C** for	**D** with
27	**A** said	**B** talked	**C** spoke	**D** told
28	**A** in	**B** at	**C** on	**D** by
29	**A** done	**B** made	**C** acted	**D** worked
30	**A** these	**B** every	**C** each	**D** this
31	**A** pleased	**B** fine	**C** clever	**D** great
32	**A** put	**B** set	**C** dial	**D** hit
33	**A** Since	**B** Because	**C** As	**D** Although
34	**A** manage	**B** find	**C** get	**D** reach
35	**A** agreeable	**B** happy	**C** grateful	**D** approving

WRITING

PART 1

Questions 1–5

- Here are some sentences about driving.
- For each question, complete the second sentence so that it means the same as the first, **using no more than three words**.
- Write only the missing words on your answer sheet.

> **Example:**   A new car is expensive to buy.
>
> **It costs a** lot of money. **to buy a new car.**

1   Large cars use more petrol than small cars.

   Small cars don't use as .... **large cars.**

2   Check your tyres before a long journey.

   Before a long journey, remember .... **your tyres.**

3   When I was young, I drove a small car.

   I used to .... **a small car when I was young.**

4   My car windscreen was broken by a stone.

   A stone .... **my car windscreen.**

5   Who does this van belong to?

   Whose .... **this?**

PART 2

Question 6

You are going to a concert this evening with a group of friends and want to ask your English friend Pat to come too.

Write a note to leave for Pat. In your note, you should

- **ask Pat to join you at the concert this evening**
- **explain where the concert will take place**
- **tell Pat what sort of music will be performed.**

Write 35–45 words on your answer sheet.

PART 3

Answer **one** of the following questions (**7** or **8**).

Question 7

- You have to write a story for your English teacher.
- Your story must begin with this sentence:

I was standing beside someone famous!

- Write your **story** in about 100 words **on your answer sheet**.

Question 8

- This is part of a letter you receive from an Australian friend.

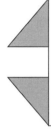

It's so hot here! What's the weather like in your country at the moment? What outdoor activities are you able to do at this time of year? Tell me about it.

- Now write a letter, answering your friend's questions.
- Write your **letter** in about 100 words **on your answer sheet**.

PAPER 2   LISTENING TEST   about 35 minutes
(including 6 minutes transfer time)

PART 1

Questions 1–7

- There are seven questions in this part.
- For each question there are three pictures and a short recording.
- Choose the correct picture and put a tick (✓) in the box below it.

Example: What's the time?

A ✓   B ☐   C ☐

1   What is the man going to buy?

A ☐   B ☐   C ☐

2   Which dress is Kate talking about?

A ☐   B ☐   C ☐

3   When will Jane meet them?

A ☐

B ☐

C ☐

4   Which morning activity is for beginners?

A ☐

B ☐

C ☐

5   Which painting does the woman decide to buy?

A ☐

B ☐

C ☐

6 What is the man selling?

A ☐ B ☐ C ☐

7 What is the weather forecast for tomorrow?

A ☐ B ☐ C ☐

PART 2

Questions 8–13

- You will hear a radio presenter talking about new books.
- For each question put a tick (✓) in the correct box.

8   To really understand *My life* you need to

A ☐ read it very slowly.

B ☐ know about the writer's life.

C ☐ read the writer's other books.

9   In *Goodbye to the fields*, John goes to London because

A ☐ his parents do not like the country.

B ☐ his father has to be close to his work.

C ☐ his parents both come from the city.

10   The *A–Z of photography* will not interest experienced photographers because

A ☐ the information is unsuitable.

B ☐ the pictures are simple.

C ☐ it says nothing about equipment.

11   The presenter likes *Cooking for one* because

A ☐ it taught her to cook Italian food.

B ☐ it contains only easy meals.

C ☐ she now likes cooking.

12 What is wrong with *Holidays in Europe*?

A ☐ It leaves out well-known places.

B ☐ The maps are not very good.

C ☐ It is too expensive.

13 Next week's programme will be useful if you

A ☐ enjoy reading reports.

B ☐ are trying to save money.

C ☐ are planning to buy presents.

PART 3

Questions 14–19

- You will hear a teacher talking about a camping trip.
- For each question, fill in the missing information in the numbered space.

Camping Trip

Coach leaves school at **(14)** .... on Monday morning.

Bring: * one bag or case

     * a **(15)** ....

     * warm clothes

     * **(16)** .... things

     * pocket money to spend on souvenirs and **(17)** ....

Catch a bus outside **(18)** .... to Southport.

Friday p.m.: Check notice board in **(19)** ....

PART 4

Questions 20–25

- Look at the six sentences for this part.
- You will hear a conversation between a girl, Lisa, and a boy, Ben, about holidays.
- Decide if each sentence is correct or incorrect.
- If it is correct, put a tick (✓) in the box under **A** for **YES**. If it is not correct, put a tick (✓) in the box under **B** for **NO**.

		A YES	B NO
20	Lisa thinks you can enjoy a holiday without spending a lot.	☐	☐
21	Ben has arranged to go on a seaside holiday.	☐	☐
22	Lisa thinks a walking holiday is healthy.	☐	☐
23	Ben thinks the weather in Scotland will be fine.	☐	☐
24	Lisa enjoys walking in hot weather.	☐	☐
25	Lisa prefers staying in hotels.	☐	☐

Visual material for the Speaking test

1B

2C

2A

2B

1C

3A

3B

4C

4A

3C

4B

4D

About the Speaking test

The Speaking test lasts about 10 to 12 minutes. You take the test with another candidate. There are two examiners in the room. One examiner talks to you and the other examiner listens to you. Both the examiners give you marks.

Part 1

The examiners introduce themselves and then one examiner asks you and your partner to say your names and spell them. This examiner then asks you questions about yourself, your daily life, interests, etc.

Part 2

The examiner asks you to talk about something together and gives you a drawing to help you.

Part 3

You each have a chance to talk by yourselves. The examiner gives you a colour photograph to look at and asks you to talk about it. When you have finished talking, the examiner gives your partner a different photograph to look at and to talk about.

Part 4

The examiner asks you and your partner to say more about the subject of the photographs in Part 3. You may be asked to give your opinion or to talk about something that has happened to you.

Test 4

PAPER 1   READING AND WRITING TEST   (1 hour 30 minutes)

READING

PART 1

QUESTIONS 1–5

- Look at the text in each question.
- What does it say?
- Mark the letter next to the correct explanation – **A**, **B** or **C** – **on your answer sheet**.

Example:

0

**NO BICYCLES
AGAINST GLASS
PLEASE**

A Do not leave your bicycle touching the window.

B Broken glass may damage your bicycle tyres.

C Your bicycle may not be safe here.

Example answer:

Part 1		
0	**A** ▬	**B** ▭ **C** ▭

1

**If red light shows, your
drink is unavailable –
please make another
choice**

A The red light goes on if the drinks machine is out of order.

B If the red light shows, you must wait before you decide on a drink.

C If the red light is on, you must choose a different drink.

2

Do not use this medicine for more than seven days without your doctor's advice

A Contact your doctor if you wish to continue using this medicine after one week.

B Doctors can only supply enough medicine for one week at a time.

C You cannot keep this medicine for more than seven days.

3

From: **Sunflowers Health Club**
To: **All Members**   Sent **15 April**
Subject: **Special Offer**

Introduce a friend to this club and receive free exercise equipment!
This offer is open to existing members; your friend must pay full 12-month fee.

A Sunflowers is selling exercise equipment to members at a special price.

B You will qualify for a gift if you persuade a friend to join Sunflowers.

C Your annual fee for Sunflowers Health Club must be paid now.

4

Please don't park within 3 metres of this vehicle – space needed for unloading

A You should not park near here because it is an exit for vehicles.

B This parking space is reserved for the vehicle's owner.

C You are requested not to park any closer than 3 metres to this vehicle.

5

This tower's in wonderful green stone, with 497 steps – stupidly, I climbed to the top! The view's supposed to be brilliant but yesterday was cloudy.
                Kenny

What did Kenny like about the tower?

A the view it gave from the top

B the material used to build it

C the number of steps it has

PART 2

Questions 6–10

- The people below all want to go for a walk.
- On the opposite page there are descriptions of eight walks.
- Decide which walk (**letters A–H**) would be the most suitable for the following people (**numbers 6–10**).
- For each of these numbers mark the correct letter **on your answer sheet**.

6   David enjoys walking but he has injured his knee and cannot climb up hills. He would like to spend a couple of hours on a quiet walk with well-marked paths.

7   Luigi likes to get as much exercise as possible and particularly likes climbing steep hills to get a good view. He wants to do a walk that is difficult and offers a range of scenery.

8   Yannis has two sons of 8 and 10. He would like to take them to see some animals in the countryside. He wants to be able to buy some refreshments.

9   Amanda has had an operation and needs plenty of fresh air to help her recover. She wants to find a short, quiet walk with a beautiful place to visit on the route.

10   Claudia's grandparents are staying with her. They are very fit and enjoy walking. They would like to visit some of the local villages and need a clearly-marked route so they don't lose their way.

WALKS FOR EVERYONE

A MILL LANE

You'll see lots of animals on this walk, because there is nothing to disturb them. Walkers often say they meet no-one. There are places where you can join or finish the walk but these are not well signposted and it is easy to get lost.

B SEA PATH

This walk starts at the village of Nye Flats and the excellent signposts lead you through local streets, fields and pretty neighbouring villages. Although it will take you half a day, there are no hills at all. You can breathe the sea air and enjoy watching traditional life in busy villages.

C CUTTERS WAY

This walk can take anything from 30 minutes to two hours. It's not a good walk for hill-lovers as the ground is completely flat, but it has good signposts and simple facilities for the hungry or thirsty walker. A few places or things to see would improve this walk, which can be a little dull.

D PADDOCK WAY

This is really a short track across a working farm. There are plenty of chickens and sheep to see, and the farmer has turned some of the buildings into an educational centre with a café. Not a walk for those who like peace and quiet, but good fun.

E HURDLES

This is a route for the experienced walker. It crosses two rivers and includes hills of up to 500 metres, from which you can see the sea. There are several rocky paths that are unsuitable for children or older people and there are no shops so take plenty of water.

F NEVERLAND

This is a walk to take if you have a whole day to spare and want to escape from other people. It follows a narrow track which is clearly marked and has different routes for different types of walker. There are hills to climb but views are limited because of thick forest.

G OVERHILL

This sounds like a difficult walk but it's really easy, although it could be better signposted. If you're a local person, you're almost certain to meet someone you know on the walk. It's a couple of kilometres outside the village of Overhill, with fields full of rabbits!

H GOLD-DIGGERS END

You won't find any gold on this peaceful walk, but you will find plenty of other things to see including a lovely garden which is open to the public. It's a half-hour walk with a couple of small cafés on the way.

PART 3

Questions 11–20

- Look at the sentences below about a theatre.
- Read the text on the opposite page to decide if each sentence is correct or incorrect.
- If it is correct, mark **A on your answer sheet**.
- If it is not correct, mark **B on your answer sheet**.

11   If a performance begins at 8 p.m., the Goddington Theatre Ticket Office
      re-opens at 7.30 that evening.

12   Bookings by credit card cost more.

13   You must pay for tickets when you reserve them.

14   Wheelchairs are allowed in front of row A.

15   The public can use the university car park at certain times only.

16   The university is on the same side of the road as the library.

17   The car park is in front of the university building.

18   You need to drive away quickly after putting your money in the car park machine.

19   The railway station is nearer the university than the bus station.

20   Taxi drivers refuse to pick up customers inside the car park.

GODDINGTON THEATRE

The Goddington Theatre Ticket Office is open from 12 noon until 4 p.m. Monday to Friday, and for half an hour in the evening before the advertised start time of each performance.

Telephone bookings

- Your tickets are held at the Ticket Office for you to collect or, if you prefer, a charge of 35p is made to post them to you. No extra charge is made for bookings by credit card.
- Reservations are held for up to four days, allowing time to call in to pay for the tickets or to send payments in the post.

Postal bookings

- You can write to the Ticket Office requesting tickets, or to confirm a reservation.

Information for the disabled

- The theatre has space for up to five wheelchairs at a performance, as the seats in positions 12–16 of row A can be removed.
- If you have difficulty with stairs, please let us know when booking.

Where to find Goddington Theatre

Goddington Theatre can be found within the Goddington University site, next to the car park, which is available for public use after 5 p.m. on weekdays and all day at weekends.

If travelling by car

Coming from the south end of Princes Street, you will see the library on your right. The next building on your right is Goddington University – there is a pedestrian crossing outside the front entrance. Take the next turning on the right after the crossing (into Broad Street) which takes you along the side of Goddington University – then first right into the car park. Drive up to the car park gate straight ahead of you, stopping as close as possible to the orange machine. Put a £1 coin in the machine and the gate will rise. (Note: Do not try to put a coin in the machine by getting out of your car – it is likely that by the time you get back in your car the gate will already be closed again!)
Other car parks are shown on the map. There is an hourly charge. You may find a free parking place on one of the side streets.

If travelling by train

You will need to allow 30 minutes to walk from the station. Taxis are available from the front of the station.

If travelling by bus/coach

The University is a 5 to 10-minute walk from the main bus station.

Taxis

When ordering a taxi from the theatre, ask to be picked up at the bottom of North Street. Taxis will not come into the car park because of the entrance charge.

PART 4

Questions 21–25

- Read the text and questions below.
- For each question, mark the letter next to the correct answer – **A**, **B**, **C** or **D** – **on your answer sheet.**

Orbis is an organisation which helps blind people everywhere. It has built an eye hospital inside an aeroplane and flown it all over the world with an international medical team. Samantha Graham, a fourteen-year-old schoolgirl from England, went with the plane to Mongolia. Samantha tells the story of Eukhtuul, a young Mongolian girl.

'Last year, when Eukhtuul was walking home from school, she was attacked by boys with sticks and her eyes were badly damaged. Dr Duffey, an *Orbis* doctor, said that without an operation she would never see again. I thought about all the everyday things I do that she couldn't, things like reading schoolbooks, watching television, seeing friends, and I realised how lucky I am.'

'The *Orbis* team agreed to operate on Eukhtuul and I was allowed to watch, together with some Mongolian medical students. I prayed the operation would be successful. The next day I waited nervously with Eukhtuul while Dr Duffey removed her bandages. "In six months your sight will be back to normal," he said. Eukhtuul smiled, her mother cried, and I had to wipe away some tears, too!'

'Now Eukhtuul wants to study hard to become a doctor. Her whole future has changed, thanks to a simple operation. We should all think more about how much our sight means to us.'

---

21   What is the writer's main purpose in writing this text?

    A   to describe a dangerous trip
    B   to report a patient's cure
    C   to explain how sight can be lost
    D   to warn against playing with sticks

22   What can a reader learn about in this text?

    A   the life of schoolchildren in Mongolia
    B   the difficulties for blind travellers
    C   the international work of some eye doctors
    D   the best way of studying medicine

23 After meeting Eukhtuul, Samantha felt

    A grateful for her own sight.
    B proud of the doctor's skill.
    C surprised by Eukhtuul's courage.
    D angry about Eukhtuul's experience.

24 What is the result of Eukhtuul's operation?

    A She can already see perfectly again.
    B After some time she will see as well as before.
    C She can see better but will never have normal eyes.
    D Before she recovers, she will need another operation.

25 Which is the postcard Samantha wrote to an English friend?

A

> I've visited a Mongolian hospital and watched local doctors do an operation.

B

> You may have to fly a long way to have the operation you need, but the journey will be worth it.

C

> I'm staying with my friend Eukhtuul, while I'm sightseeing in Mongolia.

D

> Make sure you take care of your eyes because they're more valuable than you realise!

PART 5

Questions 26–35

- Read the text below and choose the correct word for each space.
- For each question, mark the letter next to the correct word – **A**, **B**, **C** or **D** – on **your answer sheet**.

Example answer:

	Part 5			
0	A ▬	B ▭	C ▭	D ▭

The History of Film

The world's first film was shown in 1895 **(0)** .... two French brothers, Louis and Auguste Lumière. Although it only **(26)** .... of short, simple scenes, people loved it and films have **(27)** .... popular ever since. The first films were silent, with titles on the screen to **(28)** .... the story.

Soon the public had **(29)** .... favourite actors and actresses and, in this **(30)** .... , the first film stars appeared. In 1927, the first 'talkie', a film with sound, was shown and from then on, the public **(31)** .... only accept this kind of film.

Further improvements continued, particularly in America, **(32)** .... produced 95% of all films. With the arrival of television in the 1950s, **(33)** .... people went to see films, but in **(34)** .... years cinema audiences have grown again. More countries have started to produce films that influence film-making and there are currently **(35)** .... national film industries.

0	**A** by	**B** in	**C** from	**D** at
26	**A** consisted	**B** contained	**C** belonged	**D** held
27	**A** gone	**B** been	**C** made	**D** kept
28	**A** join	**B** read	**C** explain	**D** perform
29	**A** your	**B** his	**C** our	**D** their
30	**A** reason	**B** way	**C** method	**D** result
31	**A** should	**B** would	**C** might	**D** will
32	**A** who	**B** where	**C** when	**D** which
33	**A** other	**B** each	**C** fewer	**D** any
34	**A** recent	**B** now	**C** modern	**D** present
35	**A** many	**B** lots	**C** much	**D** plenty

WRITING

PART 1

Questions 1–5

- Here are some sentences about visiting a zoo.
- For each question, complete the second sentence so that it means the same as the first, **using no more than three words**.
- **Write only the missing words on your answer sheet**.

    Example: I was taken to the zoo by my friend Maria.

    My friend Maria *took me* **to the zoo.**

1   We had a map but it was difficult to find the zoo.

    Although we had a map, we .... **find the zoo easily.**

2   The car park was outside the main entrance.

    There was somewhere .... **outside the main entrance.**

3   We wore sun hats because it was very hot.

    It was .... **that we wore sun hats.**

4   Maria suggested going to see the monkeys.

    Maria said, 'Why don't we .... **the monkeys?'**

5   The elephants were my favourite animals.

    I liked the elephants .... **any other animal.**

PART 2

Question 6

Some English friends are going to visit your capital city and have asked you to recommend a hotel there.

Write an email to your friends. In your email, you should

- **say which hotel your friends should book**
- **explain why you are recommending the hotel**
- **suggest what they could do near the hotel.**

Write 35–45 words on your answer sheet.

PART 3

Answer **one** of the following questions (**7** or **8**).

Question 7

- You have to write a story for your English homework.
- Your story must have this title:

The empty house

- Write your **story** in about 100 words **on your answer sheet**.

Question 8

- This is part of a letter you receive from an English-speaking friend.

> I want to earn some money at the weekends, so I'm looking for a part-time job in a café or a shop. Which do you think would be more fun? Write soon – I need your advice!

- Now write a letter giving your friend some advice.
- Write your **letter** in about 100 words **on your answer sheet**.

PAPER 2   LISTENING TEST   about 35 minutes
                                   (including 6 minutes transfer time)

PART 1

Questions 1–7

- There are seven questions in this part.
- For each question there are three pictures and a short recording.
- Choose the correct picture and put a tick (✓) in the box below it.

Example: Where did the man leave his camera?

A ✓   B ☐   C ☐

1   Where will the woman go first after work?

A ☐   B ☐   C ☐

2   What can festival visitors see every day?

A ☐   B ☐   C ☐

3 What souvenir will the boy's mother bring?

A ☐

B ☐

C ☐

4 What time is the woman's hair appointment?

A ☐

B ☐

C ☐

5 Where's the TV guide?

A ☐

B ☐

C ☐

6 What does the man decide to take Tracy?

A ☐

B ☐

C ☐

7 Which sport has the man just started?

A ☐

B ☐

C ☐

PART 2

Questions 8–13

- You will hear a man called John Dalin talking about the travel programmes he makes for television.
- For each question, put a tick (✓) in the correct box.

8 For his most recent television
programme, John

  A ☐ drove from the North to the South Pole.

  B ☐ filmed relaxing beach holidays.

  C ☐ went to the Pacific Ocean for a year.

9 John is giving up very long trips because

  A ☐ he's too old now.

  B ☐ he's been everywhere.

  C ☐ they're too tiring.

10 John says his next television series
might be about

  A ☐ farms in Scotland.

  B ☐ old ruins in Wales.

  C ☐ cycling tours in France.

11 John wants to encourage other people to

  A ☐ be brave about travelling to new places.

  B ☐ lose their fear of flying.

  C ☐ make more trips alone.

12 Why does John want to spend more
      time near home?

    A ☐ His family might need him.

    B ☐ His wife misses him.

    C ☐ He has very young children.

13 John has already written some

    A ☐ newspaper articles.

    B ☐ travel books.

    C ☐ poems.

PART 3

Questions 14–19

- You will hear a woman talking on the radio about an exhibition of food and cooking.
- For each question, fill in the missing information in the numbered space.

The Good Food Show
at the Capital Exhibition Centre

At the show, you can

◆ buy Jane Adams' new book about making **(14)** ....

◆ get advice about buying **(15)** ....

◆ watch how to cook a lunch just with **(16)** ....

◆ learn how to make a dessert in less than **(17)** ....

◆ taste food from many different countries – the food
  from **(18)** .... is specially recommended.

The show finishes on **(19)** ....

PART 4

Questions 20–25

- Look at the six sentences for this part.
- You will hear a conversation between a teenage girl called Anna and her father about a party.
- Decide if each sentence is correct or incorrect.
- If it is correct, put a tick (✓) in the box under **A** for **YES**. If it is not correct, put a tick (✓) in the box under **B** for **NO**.

		A YES	B NO
20	Anna begins by asking her father to collect her from the party.	☐	☐
21	The party is to celebrate Tom's birthday.	☐	☐
22	Some of Tom's relations will be at the party.	☐	☐
23	Anna's father is worried about her attending the party.	☐	☐
24	Anna's father will take them to the party before the film starts.	☐	☐
25	Anna's father insists that she leaves the party at 12.00.	☐	☐

About the Speaking test

The Speaking test lasts about 10 to 12 minutes. You take the test with another candidate. There are two examiners in the room. One examiner talks to you and the other examiner listens to you. Both the examiners give you marks.

Part 1

The examiners introduce themselves and then one examiner asks you and your partner to say your names and spell them. This examiner then asks you questions about yourself, your daily life, interests, etc.

Part 2

The examiner asks you to talk about something together and gives you a drawing to help you.

Part 3

You each have a chance to talk by yourselves. The examiner gives you a colour photograph to look at and asks you to talk about it. When you have finished talking, the examiner gives your partner a different photograph to look at and to talk about.

Part 4

The examiner asks you and your partner to say more about the subject of the photographs in Part 3. You may be asked to give your opinion or to talk about something that has happened to you.

Key

PAPER 1   READING AND WRITING

READING

Part 1

1 A   2 C   3 B   4 A   5 C

Part 2

6 D   7 B   8 G   9 H   10 E

Part 3

11 B	12 B	13 A	14 A	15 A	16 B	17 A
18 B	19 A	20 A				

Part 4

21 C   22 D   23 B   24 C   25 B

Part 5

26 B	27 C	28 D	29 B	30 A	31 C	32 B
33 D	34 C	35 A				

WRITING

Part 1

1 My friend told me that I could stay in his flat.

My friend said: 'You	can stay in/at	**my flat.'**

2 I started living here two months ago.

I have lived here	since	**two months ago.**

3 This is the first time I've lived in a city.

I've	never lived	**in a city before.**

4 The flat has two bedrooms.

There	are two/2 bedrooms	**in the flat.**

5 My bedroom is too small for all my books.

My bedroom is not	large/big enough	**for all my books.**

Part 2

Task-specific Mark scheme

The content elements that need to be covered are:

i   which club you have joined
ii a suggestion that Max should join the club
iii what you can do there together

The following sample answers can be used as a guide when marking.

SAMPLE A (Test 1, Question 6: Email to Max)

> Hello Max
> I am writing to you to ask that you can join our club.
> This club is for make some foreign friends. I know that
> you want to learn French and you don't have any
> French friends. I want to learn French as well. If you join
> us you can learn French with me. I will waiting for your
> reply, bye.

Examiner Comments

All three content elements are covered appropriately and the message is clearly communicated. Candidates are not expected to include email format to get a 5.

Band: 5

SAMPLE B (Test 1, Question 6: Email to Max)

> *Hope your doing well, and I'm well too, I'm just want to inform you, I'm joined in club which it called "Blue Club" which is in Barking, so I like you to come this weekend. We are going to play pool, dancing, drinking and many more.*

Examiner Comments

In this script, all three content elements are covered and the message is communicated successfully on the whole, although the language errors require some effort by the reader.

Band: 4

SAMPLE C (Test 1, Question 6: Email to Max)

> Hi Max,
>
> I enjoy very much to invite you to go with me to the golf club next Saturday I have just found a golf club in my area and I'll be pleasure if you accept to visit the club with me. If you accept the invitation call me please.
>
> Thanks
> Vera

Examiner Comments

The first two elements are adequately dealt with, but the third (say what you could do there together) is only implied by the content of the first two elements. The message also requires some effort by the reader.

Band: 3

Part 3

The following sample answers can be used as a guide when marking.

SAMPLE D (Test 1, Question 7: Letter to a friend)

Hi Bob,

There are so many traditional festivals in my country. They depend on the area and they are different according to the season, people etc.....

The most important one of them is Da Gubal – festival. People celebrate this festival every 10th May to honor Mong-Ju princess who lived in Sila Kingdom that was name of Korea long time ago.

One day she fell in love with someone who was prince of opponent country. He loved her as well but they didn't get married. At the same time their country was in the war. He asked her to deliver information about her army.

She was worring about it. Finally she decided that she would betray him. Therefore her country won in the war

See you soon

Kim

Examiner Comments

This is a very good attempt at the task, showing confident and natural use of language. The letter is informative and requires no effort by the reader. There is a wide range of structures and vocabulary, occasionally above PET level, for example *according to the season... she would betray him.* Errors are minor, due to ambition and non-impeding, for example *that was name of Korea long time ago.*

Band: 5

SAMPLE E (Test 1, Question 7: Letter to a friend)

> Dear Jonh,
>
> I have received your letter and am very happy to get yours news. So, I want to tell you something more importante. It' is a traditional festivals in my city. Will be start on next week. It is a kind of traditional music. People are making an exibition dance with many musical instruments. I will have a good time, so I thing, I am going to take some photos for you and you can see, which impression you can do. This moment will be fantastic for verybody.
>
> I suggest you if you can come with us in this special occasion. You don't feel awful or worring about. It is a sensational african music, women are dancing a lovely song and wear sexy clothes. It is beautiful to see this spectacle in live, no, to hear. Think you very much for your letter, it is my pleasure to read you soon. Bye
> Yours friend.

Examiner Comments

This is an ambitious attempt at the task, showing some range of vocabulary. The letter has a friendly tone and gives a lot of information to the friend. However, it is flawed by a high number of mainly non-impeding errors, particularly in spelling, agreement, and use of prepositions, for example *it is a traditional festivals… this spectacle in live, no, to hear.*

Band: 3

SAMPLE F (Test 1, Question 7: Letter to a friend)

> Hello Matin,
>
> How are you? I'm fine. I want to meet you. I think we have a new years. It is the most important day. Because of they want to talking about this year's plan and didn't tell anything for a while. We would buy new cloth and meet relative and would go to grand father's tomb. If you have a festival, could you tell me something?
>
> Friendly Denny

Examiner Comments

This is a poor attempt, which is difficult to understand at times, because of impeding errors, for example *I think we have a new years. ...they want to talking about this year's plan and didn't tell anything for a while.* It is also too short at 69 words long and so receives a mark in Band 1.

Band: 1

SAMPLE G (Test 1, Question 8: Nobody knew what Adam had in his suitcase.)

> Nobody knew what adam had in his suitcase. One day, sunshine day in Brugges away to Germany adam house, he decided go to Brugges because he wrotte a poem about this place, he got the suitcase and put in, one picture he's camara, silvee neckles, a tape, two T-short, one jeans because hi's a jornalist of National Geografic, Hi like wild life, in there he met with a beautiful girl her name is Esmeralda and he asked her for the Maddison Bridge, she said is very difficult explain, I have to go with you he said ok when he got this place hi said the must beautiful I can see in my life. He said I wish take a picture with you on the Bridge, she said not I am not pretty he said I like natural impresion. She got red all face, and he said you are lady in my picture which brought in my suitcase do you want to see, look is you oh my got a can't beleve and Adam and Esmeralda lieve together for ever.

Examiner Comments

Although an ambitious attempt at story-telling, this answer is held in Band 2 because of its numerous errors, especially in sentence structure, past tenses, spelling and punctuation. Some errors impede understanding, for example *...he's camara, silvee neckles, a tape, two T-short, one jeans because hi's a ...*

Band: 2

SAMPLE H (Test 1, Question 8: Nobody knew what Adam had in his suitcase.)

> Nobody knew what Adam had in his suitcase. It was black big suitcase with silver belts he took it ever day and never left it. But the worst day for Adam have came. He lost his suitcase at the Stansted Airport. He put it only for a second and when he back the suitcase disapeared. He has looked for it everywhere but nobody saw this suitcase. Adam made a decision I had to go to police station and saw them about this case. He was very sad because it was his best suitcase like best friend and he miss a them. He was sitting at the Airport and he remembered that he had a his name address and number of his mobile phone on his suitcase. Suddenly he heard that his phone was ringing and he took it up and heard one woman had his lugage and he could took it from Hilton Hotel in London room. It was beatiful women. She sed that she didn't know how this happened but she took it Adam. Thanks you and invite her to very nice reataurant. They fall in love immidetly and got married next month. I'm this son and i tell you this story because it's very funny.
> Take care
> Dominik

Examiner Comments

This is another ambitious attempt at a story, which is longer than 100 words but not penalised for this, as the text is relevant. Some range is shown, for example *Adam made a decision… Suddenly he heard that his phone was ringing…* but there are also a high number of non-impeding errors, for example *But the worst day for Adam have came. They fall in love immidetly…*

Band: 3

SAMPLE I (Test 1, Question 8: Nobody knew what Adam had in his suitcase.)

> Nobody knew what Adam had in his suitase.
> Adam always went to somewhere with his suitcase but nobody saw when he opened it. For example he took his suitcase to work. He was a secretary and he just answered the calls. The suitcase always stood under the table at his work.
> He took the suitcase to the disco and danced near it. He always looked after the suitcase.
> And when somebody asked him what was in the suitcase he said that there was nothing interesting in the suitcase.

Examiner Comments

This is a fairly unambitious attempt, but it is virtually error-free and shows some evidence of structural range, for example ...*when somebody asked him what was in the suitcase*... . The script just reaches the minimum acceptable length of 80 words (excluding the given sentence).

Band: 4

PAPER 2   LISTENING

Part 1

1 B   2 A   3 C   4 B   5 C   6 C   7 A

Part 2

8 B   9 B   10 C   11 A   12 C   13 B

Part 3

14   Monday afternoon/p.m.
15   America / U.S.A. / United States (of America)
16   £1.75
17   tourist office(s)
18   beach
19   computer(s)

Part 4

20 B   21 A   22 A   23 B   24 A   25 A

Test 1 transcript

This is the Cambridge Preliminary English Test number 1. There are four parts to the test. You will hear each part twice.

For each part of the test, there will be time for you to look through the questions and time for you to check your answers.

Write your answers on the question paper. You will have six minutes at the end of the test to copy your answers onto the answer sheet.

The recording will now be stopped. Please ask any questions now, because you must not speak during the test.

[pause]

Now open your question paper and look at Part 1.

PART 1   *There are seven questions in this part. For each question there are three pictures and a short recording. Choose the correct picture and put a tick in the box below it.*

Before we start, here is an example.

Where did the man leave his camera?

Man: Oh no! I haven't got my camera!
Woman: But you used it just now to take a photograph of the fountain.
Man: Oh I remember, I put it down on the steps while I put my coat on.
Woman: Well, let's drive back quickly – it might still be there.

[pause]

The first picture is correct so there is a tick in box A.

Look at the three pictures for Question 1 now.

[pause]

Now we are ready to start. Listen carefully. You will hear each recording twice.

One. Which activity will the family do this year?

Woman: We're going to try an activity holiday this year, but we all want to do something different. The children want to go cycling but their father wants to go on a water sports holiday, you know, sailing and windsurfing, things like that. And I'd like to go walking. We all want to go together so we've decided to let the children choose this year, and we'll choose next year.

[pause]

Now listen again.

[The recording is repeated.]

[pause]

Two. Which is the woman's house?

Man: How will I recognise your house when I call for you, Sue?
Woman: Well, it's the same as all the others in the street, but look out for a big tree. It's by the front gate and it's covered in lovely white flowers at the moment.

[pause]

Now listen again.

[The recording is repeated.]

[pause]

Three. Why will drivers have problems this morning?

Man: And on to this morning's local traffic news. Driving conditions have improved now that the early morning fog has gone. Rain is forecast for tonight but it will be fine during the day. The police have warned drivers to expect delays coming into town because of repairs to Victoria Bridge and advise lorries to find another route if possible.

[pause]

Now listen again.

[The recording is repeated.]

[pause]

Four. What time will Robin leave the house?

Woman: Oh Robin! Pete's just rung to say that he'll be here a bit later than he said. The plane's going to take off at eight o'clock now so you don't need to check-in until about quarter past seven. He said he'd be round to pick you up at half past six instead of six o'clock. Is that OK? It'll give you some more time to pack anyway!

[pause]

Now listen again.

[The recording is repeated.]

[pause]

Five. What did Simon do this morning?

Woman: Oh Simon, you haven't even washed the dishes. Have you done anything this morning?

Boy: I've been really busy, Mum. I paid the window cleaner who called and I was going to put away all the shopping you bought yesterday but Pete rang and he kept me talking for ages.

[pause]

Now listen again.

[The recording is repeated.]

[pause]

Six. What hasn't the girl packed yet?

Woman: Have you got everything you need for your holiday?

Girl: Well, I've packed my soap and toothbrush if that's what you mean, but I can't find any toothpaste anywhere.

Woman: There's probably some in the bathroom cupboard. But what about a towel, have you remembered to pack that?

Girl: Of course.

[pause]

Now listen again.

[The recording is repeated.]

[pause]

Seven. What has the woman just bought?

Woman: What do you think? I found it in that new department store yesterday. I think it's perfect. It'll keep the sun off my face and it'll go really well with the dress I'm wearing to the wedding. It's the same colour as my bag, too. I just need a new jacket now.

[pause]

Now listen again.

[The recording is repeated.]

[pause]

That is the end of Part 1.

[pause]

PART 2   *Now turn to Part 2, questions 8–13.*

You will hear an interview with Angela Morgan, who has recently flown around the world in a helicopter.
For each question, put a tick in the correct box. You now have 45 seconds to look at the questions for Part 2.

[pause]

Now we are ready to start. Listen carefully. You will hear the recording twice.

Man: And today I'm talking to Angela Morgan. Angela, what made you decide to fly round the world in a helicopter?

Woman: People often ask me <u>why</u> I decided to do it but I'm surprised they don't ask 'Why did you wait so long?' because I'm 57 now! I'm sorry I didn't do it <u>years</u> ago, because it was such a wonderful experience. But the main purpose for going was to collect £500,000 for sick children by getting different companies to pay us money for each kilometre that we flew.

Man: And now everyone calls you the flying grandmother!

Woman: Yes, the thing about growing older is that you don't feel any different inside, so you have to do as much as you can while you can. I'm healthy, and my own children are grown up, so I was free to go.

Man: And what about preparing for the trip?

Woman: Well, it took five months to plan. I <u>was</u> going to go with my husband, but he couldn't take time off work. Instead I made the trip with my flying teacher who became a great friend while she was teaching me to fly three years ago. I passed my flying test after two weeks; found it quite easy.

Man: And what was the trip like?

Woman: It was really exciting flying over so many different countries. The only thing was that we weren't able to spend much time sightseeing because we only stopped to get water and to camp. We took very little with us, but we did have tents and cooking things to use at night. We had to spend two days in Thailand because of an engine problem, but that was the longest we spent anywhere. Fortunately nothing else went wrong, so we just kept on going after that.

Man: What did you enjoy most about the trip?

Woman: The most wonderful thing about flying was seeing the differences in the countryside as we flew across 26 countries in 97 days. We flew over oceans and close to mountains; sometimes it was quite frightening, but we didn't travel when it was dark. We spent several nights camping in the desert and the sky was just full of stars. I made a video of the trip; you'll see it in a minute.

Man: Was there anything that you missed while you were away?

Woman: Well, to my surprise I didn't miss going to work or going out to restaurants or films. The most difficult thing was sitting still all the time; I normally play tennis and swim several times a week, so I started to feel very unfit. I missed hot water and proper showers sometimes too, but not as much as I thought I would!

[pause]

Now listen again.

[The recording is repeated.]

That is the end of Part 2.

[pause]

PART 3   *Now turn to Part 3, questions 14–19.*

You will hear a radio announcer talking about activities at a museum called Science World.

For each question, fill in the missing information in the numbered space. You now have 20 seconds to look at Part 3.

[pause]

Now we are ready to start. Listen carefully. You will hear the recording twice.

Man: This week in the local activities part of the show, we're taking a look at Science World, the new place to visit for a family day out. During your visit you'll be able to find out about all the latest developments in science, as well as trying lots of experiments for yourself. This is no ordinary museum, I promise you! There's a programme of special events, which next week includes an Electricity Workshop on Monday afternoon, and the chance to do some experiments with water on Wednesday morning. Of special interest is the regular Saturday evening talk: next week Science World welcomes a famous American scientist who is going to talk about space travel.

    It isn't expensive to visit Science World, with tickets priced at three pounds for adults and two pounds for children. Talks and other special events are extra, though, with an entrance fee of £1.75 for adults and there are reductions for children. If you want to go to a special event or talk, then book your tickets direct from Science World on 284311, or pick them up from the tourist office.

    While you're at Science World, you'll be able to enjoy a snack in the Newton Café – it's a bit small, but the food is good. It's open all day and it has a lovely view because it's beside the beach.

    Still not sure? Well, why not give Science World a call on 284311? If you say you heard about Science World on this programme they will send you one free ticket to next month's exhibition which is about computers. It's suitable for families and school parties.

    And now let's look at …

[pause]

Now listen again.

[The recording is repeated.]

Key

That is the end of Part 3.

[pause]

PART 4 *Now turn to Part 4, questions 20–25.*

Look at the six sentences for this part. You will hear a conversation between a boy, Tom, and his sister, Clare, about school.
Decide if each sentence is correct or incorrect. If it is correct, put a tick in the box under A for YES. If it is not correct, put a tick in the box under B for NO. You now have 20 seconds to look at the questions for Part 4.

[pause]

Now we are ready to start. Listen carefully. You will hear the recording twice.

Boy: Guess what, Clare? I've been chosen for the school swimming team! What do you think about that?

Girl: Well, I think it's great, but I'm sure Dad won't say the same when he finds out. You know how he feels about you doing all this sport and not doing your school work. You'll never get all your homework done, especially if you have to travel to other schools for competitions.

Boy: It won't make any difference. I can do my homework on the bus.

Girl: Honestly Tom, you know what your teacher said to Dad last term. You've got a good brain and you could improve your marks at school if you spent a bit less time thinking about sport. Sometimes I wonder if you ever think about anything else at all.

Boy: Well, I work hard at everything I like doing, not just sport. I mean, take maths for example.

Girl: Okay, it's your life, but you know you have your examinations next year for college, and at most of the good colleges they have great sports facilities. If you aren't accepted, then you'll have to find a job and that won't be easy.

Boy: Oh I've thought about that already. I'm thinking of applying to do Sports Science at college and someone told me some of the colleges often take students with lower marks if they're good at sport.

Girl: Well, I wouldn't depend on what one of your friends says if I were you.

Boy: For your information it wasn't one of my friends, it was a teacher at school.

Girl: I'm only trying to help and anyway it doesn't really matter what I say, it's Dad you have to worry about.

Boy: Yes, okay. I know you're right about <u>that</u>. I'll have a chat with him tonight and explain things again.

Girl: Good luck!

[pause]

Now listen again.

[The recording is repeated.]

That is the end of Part 4.

[pause]

You now have six minutes to check and copy your answers onto the answer sheet.

Note: Teacher, stop the recording here and time six minutes. Remind students when there is **one** minute remaining.

That is the end of the test.

Test 2

PAPER 1   READING AND WRITING

READING

Part 1

1 B   2 A   3 B   4 C   5 C

Part 2

6 D   7 B   8 A   9 E   10 F

Part 3

11 A   12 A   13 B   14 A   15 B   16 A   17 B
18 A   19 B   20 A

Part 4

21 D   22 D   23 C   24 B   25 C

Part 5

26 B   27 C   28 D   29 A   30 B   31 C   32 B
33 D   34 B   35 A

WRITING

Part 1

1 Maria lives a long way from her office.

| **Maria's office isn't** | (situated/located) close to / near (to) | **her home.** |

2 It is a forty-minute bus journey to her office.

| **The bus journey to her office** | takes (her) / lasts/is (about) | **forty minutes.** |

3 Driving a car in the town centre is not allowed.

| **You are not allowed** | to drive | **cars in the town centre.** |

4 Maria sometimes takes a taxi although it is expensive.

| **Maria doesn't often take a taxi** | as/since/because | **it is expensive.** |

5 Yesterday she got up too late to catch the bus.

Yesterday she got up so late that she	missed OR didn't / couldn't / failed to catch/take/get	the bus.

Part 2

Task-specific Mark scheme

The content elements that need to be covered are:

i   an invitation to your friend to the party
ii information on when it will take place
iii a reason why you want to surprise your cousin

The following sample answers can be used as a guide when marking.

SAMPLE A (Test 2, Question 6: Card to a friend)

> Would you mind welcome to my party? This is a surprise party for my cousin. I'd like to surprise her that I'll make the big cake, and put it into the ring for present. I'll take my house and stat at 7:00 pm

Examiner Comments

All three content elements are unsuccessfully dealt with: there is no clear invitation, no explanation of why the writer wants to surprise the cousin and the information about when the party will take place only includes a time. The message also requires excessive effort to understand, for example *Would you mind welcome to my party? I'll take my house and stat at…*

Band: 1

SAMPLE B (Test 2, Question 6: Card to a friend)

Mr. Paul Dunn

Dear Paul:

I am really glad to invite you to my cousin "birthday's party". He is 6 years old and admires you a lot, because always you have been so friendly with him. The meeting will be in my house at 3:00pm. Our address is:

46 Nibthwaite Road

Harrow — Middlesex

You could take the Metro-politan line to "Harrow on the Hill" and I enclose a map if you request.

Don't forget come with your daughter Julie. Michie will have a surprise when he will see again to Julie!!!

Yours, Sincerelly

Maria Cuisans

Examiner Comments

Although the candidate has attempted the content points, the explanation why is unclear and there is inadequate information about when the party will take place. The answer is also too long due to the extra information about how to get to the house, which is irrelevant to the task set.

Band: 2

SAMPLE C (Test 2, Question 6: Card to a friend)

Dear Jim

How have you been recently? Did you remember my cousin James? Now he is ten years old. Next Sunday we will having a birthday party for him. As you know, he thinks you are the greatest magican in the whole world. So hope you can come here next Sunday. Show your fantistic magic, give him a surprise.

If you could, James must feel so happy.

Love

Tommy

Examiner Comments

This is a very good attempt, covering all content elements appropriately. Although the candidate has exceeded the word limit, the expansion is relevant to the invitation. Minor language errors are present, but do not impair the clarity of the message.

Band: 5

Part 3

The following sample answers can be used as a guide when marking.

SAMPLE D (Test 2, Question 7: Letter to a friend)

Hi I used a computer for a couple of years rather to work than play. It's helped me with my firm to account. So when I spent a lot of time face to face with a monitor I felt really upset to spent more just for a game. I'd rather prefer in my off days cycling and all activity sports My eyes need to see something more not just slashing pictures. But of course some-times when the weather is really boring (raining, winding etc) I'd like to lay at home and play to strategic game. My best is Civilisation it isn't just blood and meat everywhere. Good luck with your new amusments.
Bye, Anders

Examiner Comments

This is a good attempt, showing fairly good control and ambitious use of language. The letter is well organised on the whole and there is some evidence of range of structures and vocabulary. Errors are non-impeding, for example *I'd rather prefer in my off days... raining, winding, etc.*

Band: 4

SAMPLE E (Test 2, Question 7: Letter to a friend)

> I am very glad, that you have bought a new computer game. What's a pity, that I can not talk witch you about it!
> I don't know anything about computers, games and I don't know exactelly what is this – Play Station:). Sometimes I go to internet café in order to send e-mail to my friends and sister in Poland. I can use internet explorer and I am afraid this is all I can do with computers. And I don't like any computer games (maybe because of this I have not too much occasions to check it:).
> I prefer to write an ordinary letters like this one. In this matter I am a tradicionalist. Yours faithfully....

Examiner Comments

This is an adequate attempt at the task showing some control of language, although linking is not always maintained. There is no opening formula and a number of non-impeding errors occur, mainly in spelling and use of articles, for example *exactelly… an ordinary letters… too much occasions.*

Band: 3

SAMPLE F **(Test 2, Question 7: Letter to a friend)**

Dear Petter

I have got your letter to day at 11.30 am. How are you? Is doing fine. I am quit busy right now. I have much to do for my schoole. Soon I'll have an exame. I have to work hard in the moment. Most of time after schoole I stay in laibrery. I haven't been out since last month.

You told me that you have got a new computer game. What's it supriseing. I think that is wonderfull.

My computer is too old. It was for my brother. I am not using it often, just some times I use it for my school work. It hasn't got exciting games.

I hopp I'll get new computer soon which is letest and can use for evrything. This is my short letter, but I'll write you more next time.

Yours truly,

Yordanos

Examiner Comments

This is an inadequate attempt, which introduces substantial digression in the first half of the script before dealing with the task. It is better for candidates to focus on the topic required, rather than insert 'pre-learned' paragraphs like this. There are numerous errors, though these are mainly in spelling and are non-impeding, for example *What's it surpriseing. ...which is latest and can use for evrything.*

Band: 2

SAMPLE G **(Test 2, Question 8: Winning the prize)**

> Dear Kate:
>
> I 'am really sorry because I can't come to class this week, but I had a new for you: I tell you what happened: "I winning the prize"!!! You know, I was practising swimming a lot, this time and I had a competition in Cambrigde! The week was hardest because all our teem work lots. We were practice 4 hours per day and after out training we went to visit a lot of museums, theater, parks, etc.
>
> I enjoy that time.
>
> I hope you understand my absences but I retorn to your class again
>
> Thank you so much
>
> Maria

Examiner Comments

This is an inadequate attempt, showing some misunderstanding of the task set (the candidate has written a letter to her teacher about winning a prize). The language is fairly limited and contains numerous errors, particularly in past tenses, for example *…all our teem work lots. We were practice… I retorn to your class again.*

Band: 2

SAMPLE H **(Test 2, Question 8: Winning the prize)**

> I don't know how it happened! I have never been lucky in any lotteries, games etc. And suddenly I recived o notice from the American Ambassy that I have won a Green Card! This is impossible! One year ago I sent an application to Green Card lottery, but I didn't think about it later. I had sent it, because my friend which were with me in America told me about this, and I have known people, who had a Green card from lottery.
> This is a very nice suprise for me, because USA is my favorite place since I was there two years ago. I would never think that I could come back there.

Examiner Comments

This is a very good attempt, showing confident and ambitious use of language, with a wide range of structures and vocabulary. Errors are minor and due to this ambition, for example *…my friend which were with me in America told me about this.*

Band: 5

SAMPLE I (Test 2, Question 8: Winning the prize)

> Winning the prize. My last holiday I spent with my friends in Spain. The holiday was very, very nice. We were in Spain two weeks. Very often we went to the restaurent. Last day we went to Chine restaurent. Before I never heve been in Chine resteurent. This evening wes very excating for us. In this restaurent was the careoce. In this day someone can win the prize. The prize was a big toy. My friend Tommy is not a good singer, but he is funny. His the song wesn't well. Everybody couldn't heer him. The own of the restaurent gave him the prize, becous he wes funny. Last day in Spain I'll remember.

Examiner Comments

This is an adequate attempt, with evidence of some control of language. Simple sentence structure is sound, but there are a number of mostly non-impeding errors, especially in spelling, word order and use of articles, for example *Before I never heve been in Chine resteurent. His the song wesn't well.*

Band: 3

PAPER 2   LISTENING

Part 1

1 B   2 B   3 A   4 A   5 B   6 C   7 C

Part 2

8 A   9 C   10 C   11 A   12 A   13 C

Part 3

14   expensive / not cheap

15   Square / Sq

16   (the) (bus) driver(s)

17   map(s)

18   jewellery

19   a quarter to five / four forty(-)five / 16.45 / 4:45

Part 4

20 B   21 B   22 B   23 A   24 A   25 B

Test 2 transcript

This is the Cambridge Preliminary English Test number 2. There are four parts to the test. You will hear each part twice.

For each part of the test, there will be time for you to look through the questions and time for you to check your answers.

Write your answers on the question paper. You will have six minutes at the end of the test to copy your answers onto the answer sheet.

The recording will now be stopped. Please ask any questions now, because you must not speak during the test.

[pause]

Now open your question paper and look at Part 1.

[pause]

PART 1   *There are seven questions in this part. For each question there are three pictures and a short recording. Choose the correct picture and put a tick in the box below it.*

Before we start, here is an example.

What's the time?

Woman Have you got the time?

Man: Yes, it's twenty past three.

[pause]

The first picture is correct so there is a tick in box A.

Look at the three pictures for Question 1 now.

[pause]

Now we are ready to start. Listen carefully. You will hear each recording twice.

Key

One. How much is the man's ticket?

Man: Can you tell me how much a ticket is for Saturday's performance of Macbeth?
Woman: The front stalls and the circle are the most expensive at £16.50. The middle seats in the stalls cost £15 and the back three rows cost £12.50, but the view isn't so good. All seats are £10 for students.
Man: I'll have one in the middle please. I'm not a student. I've got my credit card here …

[pause]

Now listen again.

[The recording is repeated.]

[pause]

Two. What will they have for lunch?

Man: It's chips for lunch. What would you like with them?
Woman: Not fish again, please, and we had chicken last night.
Man: Well, we've got plenty of sausages, but we've finished the eggs, I'm afraid.
Woman: That's decided then.

[pause]

Now listen again.

[The recording is repeated.]

[pause]

Three. Why was the man late home?

Woman: Hi! Have you had a busy day at the office?
Man: Yes, sorry I'm late. I didn't get the bus because Pete offered me a lift. We didn't realise the motorway was closed because of a lorry accident, so it took much longer than normal. I'll be even later tomorrow with the train strike.

[pause]

Now listen again.

[The recording is repeated.]

[pause]

Four. What was the weather like on John's holiday?

Man 1: How was your holiday, John?
Man 2: We had a good time, but the weather was awful. We didn't have one sunny day!
Man 1: Oh dear, a week in the rain, poor you.
Man 2: Well, that's the funny thing. It never actually rained, it was just freezing cold and cloudy, we thought it might even snow.

[pause]

Now listen again.

[The recording is repeated.]

[pause]

Five. What time was the woman's appointment?

Woman: I've had an awful morning! I was really late for my hospital appointment. I just missed the 9 o'clock bus, and the next one didn't come until 20 to 10. I was supposed to see the doctor at 10 past 10, but I didn't arrive until half past. He wasn't very pleased.

[pause]

Now listen again.

[The recording is repeated.]

[pause]

Six. What did the woman buy?

Man: Did you get anything from the duty-free shop?

Woman: Well, I really wanted some of that perfume I bought last time and I got a large bottle. Then I looked for the walkman I'd promised I'd get for Tony. Fortunately, they'd sold all of them, so I had enough money for a lovely silk scarf for myself. I completely forgot about the chocolates I was supposed to get for Mary.

[pause]

Now listen again.

[The recording is repeated.]

[pause]

Seven. Where are the man and the woman talking?

Woman: It's a bit crowded isn't it … worse than a football match! Can you see well enough from here?

Man: It doesn't matter – as long as I can hear and get down the important points of what he says, it's OK.

Woman: I'm going to the library after this. I want to get this report finished so that I can go to the cinema.

[pause]

Now listen again.

[The recording is repeated.]

[pause]

That is the end of Part 1.

[pause]

PART 2   *Now turn to Part 2, questions 8–13.*

You will hear a woman called Sarah talking to a group of people about her painting.
For each question, put a tick in the correct box. You now have 45 seconds to look at the questions for Part 2.

[pause]

Now we are ready to start. Listen carefully. You will hear the recording twice.

Woman: Well, good evening everyone. I've come along to talk to you about my painting. It was just a hobby but it's really more than that now. I used to paint in the evenings after work, but now I work four days a week instead of five. That means I spend Friday, Saturday and Sunday on my painting. I have pictures in local exhibitions at least once a month.

I'd love to give up my job and spend all my time painting, but I work with computers and I earn more that way! I do make <u>some</u> money from selling my pictures, enough to pay for all my paint, brushes and paper and a few art lessons. I'd love to go to art college full-time for three years, but I've got all the rent on my flat to pay and a car to run.

I first became interested in art when I was at primary school. I used to go out with some paper and a few pencils during break time and draw anything I saw: houses, gardens, people. Then at secondary school we had art classes twice a week, and I learnt how to use chalk and then different kinds of paint: water colours, oils and so on.

Those classes were really useful for me, and ever since then I've had lessons of some kind. I've attended evening classes and been on what they call painting 'holidays', where you go out into the countryside and paint during the day and then sit and discuss your work with a teacher and the other artists after dinner. Those holidays are great; you learn so much talking to other people studying with you.

I've enjoyed painting in lots of different countries. I've been to Morocco and painted desert scenes with beautiful sunrises. I've been to Greece and Spain and painted pictures of the local people working in the fields near their homes. My favourite place is still Scotland. I love walking in the Scottish mountains, and there are so many different birds to see, especially in spring.

Well, I'm going to finish now by showing you a video of the places I've visited. After that there'll be a chance to relax with a cup of coffee and then there'll be time for some questions. Oh, and I've got some information about my next art exhibition for you. It's going to be at the Queen's Gallery. Now, if someone would turn off the lights …

[pause]

Now listen again.

[The recording is repeated.]

That is the end of Part 2.

[pause]

PART 3   *Now turn to Part 3, questions 14–19.*

You will hear a radio programme giving you information about the city of Glasgow.
For each question, fill in the missing information in the numbered space. You now have 20 seconds to look at Part 3.

[pause]

Now we are ready to start. Listen carefully. You will hear the recording twice.

Man: Well, good morning. This week's programme is about the city of Glasgow. We're going to give you some ideas of what you can see and do if you visit for a weekend. Glasgow is Britain's third largest city, and Scotland's biggest. It is well worth a visit.

If you arrive by car, the motorway will take you into the city centre. Don't park in one of the city centre car parks however, as they are expensive. It's better to leave your car at your hotel or somewhere away from the centre, and take the bus.

Glasgow is a large city and there is an excellent public transport system. A good idea is to catch a "Discovering Glasgow" tour bus which leaves George Square every half hour. You can get off anywhere and catch the next bus to continue your trip. The tour costs £5 and tickets are available from the bus driver.

If you want to walk around the city centre, then it's best to start at the Welcome Centre on St Vincent Place. You can get information about opening times and entrance fees of places to visit and take a free map to help you with your sightseeing.

Don't miss the fifteenth century cathedral, which has particularly beautiful windows. Further on is the Merchant City area, where there are cafés and lots of small, fashionable shops which sell jewellery and clothes.

Byres Road is popular with university students and you can find a lot of bargains in the shops around there. The Botanic Gardens are also worth a visit. The gardens are open until sunset, and the glasshouses from ten o'clock until a quarter to five. These contain a wide variety of beautiful plants and flowers. The gardens are also a good place to have a picnic.

Well …

[pause]

Now listen again.

[The recording is repeated.]

That is the end of Part 3.

[pause]

PART 4   *Now turn to Part 4, questions 20–25.*

Look at the six sentences for this part. You will hear a conversation between a boy, Frank, and a girl, Linda, in a music shop.
Decide if each sentence is correct or incorrect. If it is correct, put a tick in the box under A for YES. If it is not correct, put a tick in the box under B for NO. You now have 20 seconds to look at the questions for Part 4.

[pause]

Now we are ready to start. Listen carefully. You will hear the recording twice.

Boy: So, where do you want to go first, Linda?
Girl: Let's go in here. I want to see what they've got. It was my birthday last week and Mum gave me some cassettes. They're really great but I've already got one of them so I want to change it for something else.
Boy: I love this shop, there's always so much to choose from. What are you going to get?
Girl: I'm not sure. I thought I'd just have a look around and see if there's anything I like the look of. I want something different. I'm a bit bored with all the music I normally listen to. Can you suggest anything?
Boy: Well, you don't usually like the sort of music I listen to. What about this band?
Girl: Who are they? I've never heard of them.
Boy: They're a new band from America. They're not very well known yet but you wait and see. In another couple of years they'll be really famous.
Girl: Mmm, let me have a look. Can you find it on cassette for me? I haven't got a CD player.
Boy: The sound's much better on a CD, you should get one.
Girl: Well, there's no point for me, my cassette player's really good quality, so it wouldn't make any difference. Besides CDs cost a lot more than cassettes.
Boy: Here you are. I've found it on cassette.
Girl: Oh look, it's on special offer. That's really cheap, isn't it? I'll take it.
Boy: There's something else we could get while we're here.

Girl: What's that?

Boy: Well, there's a concert in the sports stadium next week. There's a new Irish band playing. You might like them, so would you like to come with me?

Girl: That sounds great. I hope I do like them. The last band you took me to see was awful.

Boy: This one is different. I'll go and buy some tickets then, shall I?

Girl: All right then.

[pause]

Now listen again.

[The recording is repeated.]

That is the end of Part 4.

[pause]

You now have six minutes to check and copy your answers onto the answer sheet.

Note: Teacher, stop the recording here and time six minutes. Remind students when there is **one** minute remaining.

That is the end of the test.

Test 3

PAPER 1   READING AND WRITING

READING

Part 1

1 C   2 B   3 B   4 A   5 C

Part 2

6 E   7 A   8 C   9 F   10 G

Part 3

11 A   12 B   13 A   14 A   15 A   16 A   17 A
18 B   19 B   20 B

Part 4

21 A   22 C   23 D   24 B   25 C

Part 5

26 C   27 D   28 B   29 A   30 A   31 D   32 C
33 B   34 C   35 C

WRITING

Part 1

1 Large cars use more petrol than small cars.

Small cars don't use as	much petrol as	large cars.

2 Check your tyres before a long journey.

Before a long journey, remember	to check	your tyres.

3 When I was young, I drove a small car.

I used to	drive	a small car when I was young.

4 My car windscreen was broken by a stone.

A stone	broke	my car windscreen.

5 Who does this van belong to?

Whose	van is	this?

Part 2

Task-specific Mark scheme

The content elements that need to be covered are:

i   a request for Pat to join you at the concert this evening
ii information on where the concert will take place
iii information about what sort of music will be performed

The following sample answers can be used as a guide when marking.

SAMPLE A (Test 3, Question 6: Note to Pat)

> Hi Pat,
> I am going to invite you go to a concert with me this evening. The concert place just near your house. Can you wait for me in the xxx street? Pop music will be performed. I'm hoping you enjoy it.
> Your friend
> Jiang
> Nov 20th

Examiner Comments

All three content elements are adequately dealt with and the message is communicated successfully on the whole, but language errors require a little effort by the reader.

Band: 4

SAMPLE B (Test 3, Question 6: Note to Pat)

> Do you have a plenty of time this evening? Because I am going to go to a concert this evening with a group of friends and I want to you come too.
>
> When you will go there with me maybe you will have a nice time. You take a 6 of bus and then come to the Picadilly tube station. We are waiting for you until 7.00pm. I don't know but someone said to me they have got perfect harmoney.

Examiner Comments

This is an inadequate attempt, as the candidate has responded to the bullet points instead of writing a cohesive note to a friend, which leads to only partial realisation of the task (the second and third elements are unsuccessfully addressed).

Band: 2

SAMPLE C (Test 3, Question 6: Note to Pat)

> Hello Pat! I and some friends are going to a concert tonight. I let you this message to ask you to join us. The concert will take place at Stratford's shopping centre at 9pm. It will be a Jazz concert
>
> See you tonight!

Examiner Comments

All content elements are covered appropriately in a clearly communicated message. Language errors are minor and require no effort by the reader.

Band: 5

Part 3

The following sample answers can be used as a guide when marking.

SAMPLE D (Test 3, Question 7: I was standing beside someone famous!)

> I was standing beside someone famous! I was so excited that during a few seconds I couldn't do anything. I was standing and loocked him. He was more taller and more beautiful that he seemed on TV.
>
> Suddenly he turned his head and fixed me. I was petrified! He smiled and said hello. I opened my mouth but I couldn't say something. He asked me how I found the show. Finaly I answered him. I said it was great. I added that I loved his music and particular his last album. I asked him to sign me an autograph the he shaked my hand and went.

Examiner Comments

This is a very good attempt, showing confident use of language and a wide range of vocabulary, for example *Suddenly he turned his head... I was petrified*. Errors are minor and mostly due to ambition, for example *I added that I loved his music and particular his last album*. The story is also well organised and requires no effort to read.

Band: 5

SAMPLE E (Test 3, Question 7: I was standing beside someone famous!)

> I was standing beside someone famous! I could't belive! I was doing the shopping, like every Saturday, you know boring life.....But in one time I see Madonna is trying new dress! First time I thout. No it's impossible! Madonna doing shoping in the same Supermarket like me?! But it was trou! She came for the premiere new Band! It was emaising! First time in my life I'm met someon famous! (exclusive TV). This boring day was changing and stay one of the most exciting in my life! No I know every next day can give me someting new, very interesting experience. I'm very happy I arrived to London! This is fantastic city!

Examiner Comments

This is an ambitious and lively attempt at telling a story, which is flawed by a number of mostly non-impeding errors, for example *I could't belive… Madonna is trying new dress. It was emaising!* Two errors impede understanding: *(exclusive TV)… No I know every next day…*

Band: 3

SAMPLE F (Test 3, Question 7: I was standing beside someone famous!)

> I was standing beside someone famous!
> It was long tome ago I saw o the strreet Elton Jon I
> was suprice, and shocked because he set hello to me
> and how are you, he was really friendli, I don't now way
> I felt sow heppe because I met someon famous.
> London is a very big city, is posible to see e lot of
> famous pepul.

Examiner Comments

This is an inadequate attempt, which is only 60 words long. The language is fairly limited and repetitive, and errors often occur in the spelling of PET-level words, for example *he set hello... I felt sow heppe... famous pepul.*

Band: 2

SAMPLE G **(Test 3, Question 8: Letter to a friend)**

Hi! How are you? Are you all right? I'm fine. Is it very hot in Australia now? Now my country is coming the winter. It is cold everyday. I went to Mt. Fuji last week. It was very very cold. But I enjoyed to climb up Mt. Fuji! After 2 months, I will go to snow mountains because I can play "Snow board". When I was 17 years old I begun to play it. I can play it very well I think. I have never been in Australia but I watched on TV about Australia. I think Australia is hot whole year! Is this truth? Please tell me and I have never played surfing please teach me. I'd like to play surfing! If you could to Japan, I can take you all Japan. Now Japan is fall! I want t take to the mountains because it is very beautiful the mountains. The leaf is changing from green to red or yellow! Can you imagine like New England area? The same! Anyway I enjoy to go all of Japan. Have a good time. I hope you will be happy! Take care! Bye!

Examiner Comments

This is a good attempt at writing a detailed and friendly letter. There is fairly good control of language and evidence of range, especially some relevant vocabulary. Errors are non-impeding, for example *Now my country is coming the winter... I'd like to play surffing.*

Band: 4

SAMPLE H (Test 3, Question 8: Letter to a friend)

Hello Thomas, I was very glad when I recieved your letters from Australia. I haven't heard from you for a long time. How are you? Did you find a new job? How are you getting on? At home in Hungary there is nothing specially. I'm sure the whether better there than here. Two weeks before was snowing and the life is stopped. This was the first time where was snowing. At the moment there is no snow inlead always raining. Therfore we can't do any outdoor activities. Only indoors. For example we can go to swim in the swiming pool or play squash in the fitness center. But do you now I every day go to airobic, of course in week days. I hope you can do more outdoors activities. It's more healthy.

Sorry, but I have to finish my letter I promise the next time I'll write more.

Your friend, Jud

Examiner Comments

This is an adequate attempt, showing some control of language. Simple sentence structure is sound, although there are a number of mostly non-impeding errors, for example *I'm sure the whether better there than here... But do you now I every day go to airobic...* The answer requires some effort by the reader.

Band: 3

SAMPLE I (Test 3, Question 8: Letter to a friend)

> *Whats's the weather hir? Rain, rain, rain!*
>
> *Every morning when I wake up see the same!*
>
> *I love sun but....*
>
> *I don't know what write to you about activities which I'm going to do outdoor? When is weather like now I need only sleep! When I get up in the morning I think only about when I come bek to my bed! What you thin about it? Mayby I have go to the doctor?*

Examiner Comments

This is an inadequate attempt, which is slightly short at 76 words and has no opening or closing formulae. There are some non-impeding errors in word order, question formation, use of articles and spelling, for example *When is weather like now... What you thin about it? Mayby I have go to the doctor?*

Band: 2

Key

Part 1

1 B   2 C   3 C   4 B   5 A   6 A   7 A

Part 2

8 C   9 B   10 A   11 C   12 B   13 C

Part 3

14   (0)7.45
15   sleeping bag / sleep bag
16   swimming / swim
17   drink(s)
18   Post Office
19   (college) entrance hall

Part 4

20 A   21 B   22 A   23 B   24 B   25 B

Test 3 transcript

This is the Cambridge Preliminary English Test number 3. There are four parts to the test. You will hear each part twice.

For each part of the test, there will be time for you to look through the questions and time for you to check your answers.

Write your answers on the question paper. You will have six minutes at the end of the test to copy your answers onto the answer sheet.

The recording will now be stopped. Please ask any questions now, because you must not speak during the test.

[pause]

Now open your question paper and look at Part 1.

[pause]

PART 1   *There are seven questions in this part. For each question there are three pictures and a short recording. Choose the correct picture and put a tick in the box below it.*

Before we start, here is an example.

What's the time?

Woman: Have you got the time?
Man: Yes, it's twenty past three.

[pause]

The first picture is correct so there is a tick in box A.

Look at the three pictures for Question 1 now.

[pause]

Now we are ready to start. Listen carefully. You will hear each recording twice.

One. What is the man going to buy?

Woman: Is everything ready for the holiday?

Man: I'm just going shopping – I must get those pills I take when I feel travel sick. Do we need anything else at the chemist's? We forgot the toothpaste last time!

Woman: I've got that. I haven't got any sunglasses, but I can borrow yours, can't I? And I'll get something to read at the airport.

Man: Right.

[pause]

Now listen again.

[The recording is repeated.]

[pause]

Two. Which dress is Kate talking about?

Girl: Oh Mum, this dress is still dirty!

Woman: It can't be, Kate – I've only just washed it.

Girl: Well it is. The mark on the collar has gone, but there's still a small one here – look it's at the front just below the button. It's where I spilt some Coke last week.

[pause]

Now listen again.

[The recording is repeated.]

[pause]

Three. When will Jane meet them?

Man: Hi, it's Pete here. Jane left a message to say she can't meet us at 8.00 as planned, because her bus doesn't get in till 8.15 and it'll take her 30 minutes to get from the centre of town. I told her the table is actually booked for 8.45 so that would be fine and we'll see her then.

[pause]

Now listen again.

[The recording is repeated.]

[pause]

Four. Which morning activity is for beginners?

Man: At 10.00 a.m. tomorrow morning there will be swimming lessons, at both intermediate and beginner level. Then there will be volleyball practice at 11.30 for all those of you who are already in one of the teams. Also in the morning, for those of you who already know how to sail, there's a chance to do some practice on your own. There will be lessons in both sailing and windsurfing for beginners after lunch.

[pause]

Now listen again.

[The recording is repeated.]

[pause]

Five. Which painting does the woman decide to buy?

Woman: They're all nice, but you see a lot of flowers everywhere these days, don't you, so that wouldn't be my choice. The same goes for animals actually, although I do quite like the one of the horses. So, it looks like it'll have to be the one with the boats. It will be a change from that bowl of fruit I've had on the wall all these years, anyway.

[pause]

Now listen again.

[The recording is repeated.]

[pause]

Six. What is the man selling?

Man: And this is the latest model by Macpoint. You'll find it's even quicker at doing your washing up and needs less water. And it's very easy to use – as easy as turning on your shower.

[pause]

Now listen again.

[The recording is repeated.]

[pause]

Seven. What is the weather forecast for tomorrow?

Woman: … it's been typical spring weather today, sunshine and showers. The next twenty-four hours should be dry but cloudy … Things look better for the next week, with Monday being a fine sunny day and the following day mild but windy …

[pause]

Now listen again.

[The recording is repeated.]

[pause]

That is the end of Part 1.

[pause]

PART 2　　*Now turn to Part 2, questions 8–13.*

You will hear a radio presenter talking about new books.
For each question, put a tick in the correct box. You now have 45 seconds to look at the questions for Part 2.

[pause]

Now we are ready to start. Listen carefully. You will hear the recording twice.

Woman: Welcome to this week's book programme. We've got lots of great new books to tell you about.
　　My life, by Joe Wrigley, will keep all fans of Joe's stories happy for hours. It explains a lot about where his ideas come from and gives a picture of what was happening in his life when he was working on his most successful books. I must say, though, that some of it is difficult to understand if you haven't read his other books.

Now, for those of you who like a good cry, *Goodbye to the fields*, by Susan Marks, tells the sad story of John, a small boy who has to leave the countryside he loves when the family move to London because of his father's job. John and his mother would prefer to stay where they are. It's a long time before the family begins to feel comfortable living in the big city.

There are plenty of books with helpful advice this week. First, the *A–Z of photography* would make a great present for anyone just starting out with a camera. It has everything you need to know to take really good photos, and learn about cameras, film, lighting and so on. This is not one for the experienced photographer, though – there's not much advanced information here.

Turning to the kitchen, *Cooking for one*, by Adrian White, says on its cover that even people who hate cooking will find it useful. A month ago, I couldn't even boil an egg, but now I'm producing all sorts of dishes, some quite difficult, and, yes, they taste quite good, too. I'm actually enjoying cooking now. I'm now going to try a new book about cooking Italian food.

The last book this week is *Holidays in Europe*, by Mary Curtis. This is an enjoyable read, which will start your imagination working as you plan for next year's holiday. It doesn't matter that the writer doesn't talk about the famous places everyone visits, but describes lots of small places away from the main tourist areas. The maps are too small to be useful but the book is still good value for money.

That's it for this week, then. Next week, there's a special report on giving books as presents, so if you've saved up your money and you're wondering what to get for a friend or relation for their birthdays, you might get some good ideas … I'll look forward to talking to you then …

[pause]

Now listen again.

[The recording is repeated.]

That is the end of Part 2.

[pause]

PART 3   *Now turn to Part 3, questions 14–19.*

You will hear a teacher talking about a camping trip.
For each question, fill in the missing information in the numbered space. You now have 20 seconds to look at Part 3.

[pause]

Now we are ready to start. Listen carefully. You will hear the recording twice.

Man: Thank you all for coming. I'm going to give you the final details of our camping trip next week. You may like to make some notes as there's a lot to remember.

The coach will be outside the school on Monday morning at 7.30 and we will set off at 7.45 so don't be late. There'll be room on the coach for one bag each so please don't bring more than one bag or suitcase. You don't need to bring tents or food as that's all provided for us, but you will need to bring a sleeping bag. It turns cold at night so bring some warm clothes too. If we're lucky though, the sun will shine and we'll be able to use the outdoor pool on the site so don't forget your swimming things.

On to pocket money – please don't bring too much. We can't keep a lot of money safe. £5 per day should be plenty so you can buy souvenirs and drinks while we are out visiting places.

You will probably also want to bring some extra money for the last day when you are free. The campsite is in the middle of the countryside so if you've had enough fresh air by then, you may want to go shopping in the nearest town about eight miles away. That's Southport. There's plenty to do there and there's a bus that stops outside the Post Office in the village down the road. I'll point it out to you when we get there.

On Friday afternoon, before you leave college, please look at the notice board in the entrance hall as there may be some changes to the arrangements which I need to tell you about.

Now, has anyone got any questions?

[pause]

Now listen again.

[The recording is repeated.]

That is the end of Part 3.

[pause]

PART 4 *Now turn to Part 4, questions 20–25.*

Look at the six sentences for this part. You will hear a conversation between a girl, Lisa, and a boy, Ben, about holidays.
Decide if each sentence is correct or incorrect. If it is correct, put a tick in the box under A for YES. If it is not correct, put a tick in the box under B for NO. You now have 20 seconds to look at the questions for Part 4.

[pause]

Now we are ready to start. Listen carefully. You will hear the recording twice.

Girl: Hi, Ben! Only one more week at college, and then the summer holidays begin. Great, isn't it!

Boy: I don't know. It might get a bit boring. I don't think I've got enough money to go anywhere nice for a holiday this year.

Girl: It <u>would</u> be nice to have lots of money to spend but a good holiday doesn't have to be expensive!

Boy: Oh yes it does! The best holiday I ever had was a few years ago when I went to Greece. I want to fly off somewhere hot, and lie on the beach and go swimming.

Girl: Yes, well, I can't afford to do that, either.

Boy: So what are you doing this summer?

Girl: I'm going on a walking holiday in Scotland with some friends. We went last year, and we really enjoyed it. We walked all day and spent the nights in Youth Hostels. Why don't you come with us? We're going for two weeks. It won't cost much, and you'll come home feeling really relaxed and fit.

Boy: I'm not sure. Walking all day sounds like hard work to me. And surely you're not hoping for lots of sunshine in Scotland?

Girl: It did rain a bit last year, but most of the time it was sunny. Anyway, it's not good walking in the heat. You have to stop all the time to rest and have drinks.

Boy: Well, I like the sun, and I like to stay in comfortable hotels, not Youth Hostels!

Girl: But they <u>are</u> comfortable. They're basic, and the food's often not very good, but they're very clean and cheap. In fact I prefer them to hotels because the people are always so friendly.

Boy: Maybe. Look Lisa, thanks a lot for asking me, but I think I'll just stay home and get bored!

[pause]

Now listen again.

[The recording is repeated.]

That is the end of Part 4.

[pause]

You now have six minutes to check and copy your answers onto the answer sheet.

Note: Teacher, stop the recording here and time six minutes. Remind students when there is **one** minute remaining.

That is the end of the test.

Test 4

PAPER 1   READING AND WRITING

READING

Part 1

1 C   2 A   3 B   4 C   5 B

Part 2

6 C   7 E   8 D   9 H   10 B

Part 3

11 A   12 B   13 B   14 B   15 A   16 A   17 B
18 A   19 B   20 A

Part 4

21 B   22 C   23 A   24 B   25 D

Part 5

26 A   27 B   28 C   29 D   30 B   31 B   32 D
33 C   34 A   35 A

WRITING

Part 1

1 We had a map but it was difficult to find the zoo.

Although we had a map, we	couldn't / could not / didn't / did not	**find the zoo easily.**

2 The car park was outside the main entrance.

There was somewhere	to park	**outside the main entrance.**

3 We wore sun hats because it was very hot.

It was	so (very) hot/sunny	**that we wore sun hats.**

4 Maria suggested going to see the monkeys.

Maria said, 'Why don't we	go to/and see	**the monkeys?'**

5 The elephants were my favourite animals.

I liked the elephants	more/better than	any other animal.

Part 2

Task-specific Mark scheme

The content elements that need to be covered are:

i   a suggestion for which hotel your friend should book
ii   an explanation of why you are recommending the hotel
iii a suggestion as to what they could do near the hotel

The following sample answers can be used as a guide when marking.

SAMPLE A (Test 4, Question 6: Email to friends)

> Dear friends
>   Before you are going to visit my country, you'd book the most famous hotel of my country, because the hotel has nice food, view and many famous places near by the hotel. By the way, the hotel is nearly my house, so I think you'd book the hotel. I hope to see you soon
>
> Love from
> Hao

Examiner Comments

This is an inadequate attempt, which fails to name the hotel and barely addresses the final point, as no suggestion is made. The writer's friends could make little practical use of the email.

Band: 2

SAMPLE B (Test 4, Question 6: Email to friends)

Hello Sean,

I am very happy because you and Ronan are coming to Mexico, I think that to stay in the Royal Palace Hotel is the best option, I recommend that hotel because is in the centre of the city, is quite nice and not very expensive.

If you like to go for a walk and to know about our culture, this hotel is the best, because everything is near.

You can book the hotel on www.theroyalhotel.com.mx.

Love from

Mayra

Examiner Comments

All content elements are covered appropriately and the message is clearly communicated, with minimal errors. At 75 words, the answer is longer than necessary but has not been penalised, as all the information is relevant to the readers. However, candidates should be trained to observe the word limits.

Band: 5

SAMPLE C (Test 4, Question 6: Email to friends)

You should book the Ebisu-garden Hotel. Because you can get anywhere easilier from Ebisu.

The Ebisu-garden Hotel was built about five years ago. It has a lot of new things there. It is popular in famous people. A lots of famous people from over the world have been stayed there.

Examiner Comments

In this script, the first two content elements are covered appropriately, but the third element has been omitted. The script can only receive 3, therefore. Language errors do not affect the clarity of the message.

Band: 3

Part 3

The following sample answers can be used as a guide when marking.

SAMPLE D (Test 4, Question 7: The empty house)

The empty house

That history began when one day a woman who lived in a very big house in Oxford had to move to another city. So she was taking off her furniture from the house during three days, but the last day she fell down the stairs and she died so the house was along and never nobody was to live at this home. Some times some neighbours went at that house but they said that they could see the house with all the furniture in the same place, but when they went at night the woman apeaieced taking off the furniture and the house was empty, the children thought it was the woman's phanto.

Examiner Comments

This is a good attempt at a story, which is well organised and shows some range of structures and vocabulary (the first sentence is particularly good). There is fairly good control, though some non-impeding errors occur as a result of ambition, for example *...she was taking off her furniture.*

Band: 4

SAMPLE E (Test 4, Question 7: The empty house)

> When I stay in my home, I remember the teacher told me "You need to do your English homework", so when I starded to do my homework while I was listening footstops, I'm very afraid and in that moment I'm call the police, and the police ask me "what happend are you ok and I said, please come and help me because I'm alone in my house and I think one person try to kill me.
>
> In that moment I'm very scared and then I don't remember anything, when I woke up this morning all things are ok, but I don't have to do my homework, so I think the teacher's never have do English homework because every time something is wrong.

Examiner Comments

Although the candidate has tried hard to produce a story, the numerous errors make it difficult to follow and require considerable effort by the reader. Past tenses are problematic, for example *I'm call the police, and the police ask me "what happend…"*.

Band: 2

SAMPLE F **(Test 4, Question 7: The empty house)**

> The empty house
> One day when I got home I didn't find anything,
> unfurtinatly my house was stolen. It is thought that the
> robe was made at Mid-day when I was out, However
> some neighbours of mine saw the people that made it.
> Now the police is investigating the clues and I have to
> wait for the answer.
> I was very sad because sadenly somebody robe your
> things which you had got with hours of hard work and
> now you have to start again.
> Is life!!!
> What I mean is please be carefull with your owns things
> because always someone is waiting to robe you.

Examiner Comments

This answer contains a number of non-impeding errors but at the same time, there is some range of language, such as *investigating the clues...* and some control of more complex sentences, for example *However some neighbours of mine saw the people that ....* The candidate has problems with the commonly confused words *do/make* and *rob/burgle/steal*.

Band: 3

SAMPLE G (Test 4, Question 8: Letter to a friend)

Dear Friend

I think, if you looking for a part-time job is very good option, I think the best place is in a café because you meet a lot of people and you received more money and the job is very hard but in my opion is a good job.

You need think about what do you want? And of course wich place do you like more. If you acepted the job it's very good because you have your own money and you no't necesary dependent of your parent. I hope you choice the best option and enjoy this job.

With love

Vanessa Candioti

Examiner Comments

This is a borderline Band 2/3 script but the numerous errors, particularly in tense formation and the spelling of PET-level words, place it in Band 2, for example *If you looking for... in my opion... . I hope you choice...* . The candidate also has problems with modal verbs, for example *You need think about...* . The organisation of the letter is quite good and with better control, the candidate would have scored a higher mark.

Band: 2

SAMPLE H (Test 4, Question 8: Letter to a friend)

Hello,

I have recieved your letter and knowed you are going to find a job if I were you I would get a job in the café than a shop following two reasons.

Firstly, in the café the etomosphere is more friendly than shop because most of people who go to café just want to relax and they almost very happy. So you can easy to talk with them and make even friends with them.

Secondly you can work in the café in the night and avoid have impact with your course. After study hard in the daytime you can relax in the café and also can get money. I think it's fit for you who don't stay at home in the night.

Ok, that is my advice for you but decide by yourself.

Hope you can find a good part-time job.

Examiner Comments

This answer is ambitious and fluent, showing some range of structures and vocabulary, such as *if I were you I would get...* . However, it is flawed by a number of mainly non-impeding errors, for example *the etomosphere is more friendly than shop... After study hard in the daytime...* .

Band: 3

SAMPLE I (Test 4, Question 8: Letter to a friend)

Dear Hazel

I want to tell you something, if you want fun; you have to look for a job in a café because in cafes always there are a lot of young people and sometimes they are looking for new friends and you can meet new people every weekend. This is my advice, I think that if you get a job in a café, you will be very happy.

Another good thing about working in a café is the money, you will earn more money in a café than in a shop.

I hope you are fine and I am sure, you will make the best deccission and you will do very well.

I love you

Mayra

Examiner Comments

The candidate has produced a competent and friendly letter. There is generally good control and effective linking, for example *Another good thing about working in a café… .* Errors are minor and occur mainly in spelling. The answer would receive a low Band 5 mark, due to the absence of vocabulary range.

Band: 5

PAPER 2   LISTENING

Part 1

1 B   2 B   3 C   4 A   5 C   6 B   7 C

Part 2

8 C   9 C   10 B   11 A   12 A   13 B

Part 3

14 cakes
15 (fresh) fish
16 vegetables
17 15/fifteen minutes
18 Canada
19 23 March

Part 4

20 B   21 B   22 A   23 B   24 B   25 A

Test 4 transcript

This is the Cambridge Preliminary English Test number 4. There are four parts to the test. You will hear each part twice.

For each part of the test, there will be time for you to look through the questions and time for you to check your answers.

Write your answers on the question paper. You will have six minutes at the end of the test to copy your answers onto the answer sheet.

The recording will now be stopped. Please ask any questions now, because you must not speak during the test.

[pause]

Now open your question paper and look at Part 1.

[pause]

PART 1   *There are seven questions in this part. For each question there are three pictures and a short recording. Choose the correct picture and put a tick in the box below it.*

Before we start, here is an example.

Where did the man leave his camera?

Man: Oh no! I haven't got my camera!
Woman: But you used it just now to take a photograph of the fountain.
Man: Oh I remember, I put it down on the steps while I put my coat on.
Woman: Well, let's drive back quickly – it might still be there.

[pause]

The first picture is correct so there is a tick in box A.

Look at the three pictures for Question 1 now.

[pause]

Now we are ready to start. Listen carefully. You will hear each recording twice.

One. Where will the woman go first after work?

Man: Are you and Sarah going straight to the restaurant from work tonight?

Woman: Actually, I'm leaving work early because I need to do some shopping in the market, and I'm going to meet Sarah after that outside the cinema. She doesn't know where the restaurant is, you see. You're playing tennis after work, aren't you?

Man: Yes. So I'll see you at the restaurant.

[pause]

Now listen again.

[The recording is repeated.]

[pause]

Two. What can festival visitors see every day?

Woman: The Arts Centre in London is holding a festival of Irish culture from the 4th to 12th of April. An exhibition of paintings is open daily and on some weekday evenings the Theatre has special events including plays and films. At the weekend, concerts of Irish music will take place in the Town Hall.

[pause]

Now listen again.

[The recording is repeated.]

[pause]

Three. What souvenir will the boy's mother bring?

Woman: What colour T-shirt shall I bring you from New York, Fred?

Boy: I'd prefer black but … actually a baseball cap would be a good idea.

Woman: Mmm. Or what about another model car for your collection? I could get you a New York taxi.

Boy: Great. I really liked the sports car you bought me last time.

[pause]

Now listen again.

[The recording is repeated.]

[pause]

Four. What time is the woman's hair appointment?

Woman 1: I'd like to make an appointment to have my hair cut please. This Friday or Saturday in the morning if you can manage it.

Woman 2: Let me see … we can do Friday at 10.00 or 11.30, then on Saturday there's 9.30 or 12 o'clock.

Woman 1: I'll take the earlier one on Saturday please.

[pause]

Now listen again.

[The recording is repeated.]

[pause]

Five. Where's the TV guide?

Woman: Have you seen the TV guide?

Boy: Isn't it on top of the television? I had it when I was watching the film last night.

Woman: I expect you left it by your chair then. Here it is under the cushion where nobody can find it. You should put it back in its place by the telephone. Then we'd all know where it is.

[pause]

Now listen again.

[The recording is repeated.]

[pause]

Six. What does the man decide to take Tracy?

Man: I'm going to see Tracy in hospital, but I can't think of what to take her. People always take flowers …

Woman: … so she'll have lots already for sure. I always think it's nice to have something to read myself, but as Tracy's got her walkman with her, what about something to listen to?

Man: What a good idea. It's better than taking sweets, certainly, because I know she's on a special diet while she is in hospital.

[pause]

Now listen again.

[The recording is repeated.]

[pause]

Seven. Which sport has the man just started?

Woman: Hi, how was your holiday?

Man: Great, really good windsurfing and sailing – you know how much I enjoy them. And horse-riding … I really want to go again now I've tried it. And the swimming pool was wonderful too – much warmer than the one I usually swim in … holidays are just too short!

[pause]

Now listen again.

[The recording is repeated.]

[pause]

That is the end of Part 1.

[pause]

PART 2   *Now turn to Part 2, questions 8–13.*

You will hear a man called John Dalin talking about the travel programmes he makes for television.
For each question, put a tick in the correct box. You now have 45 seconds to look at the questions for Part 2.

[pause]

Now we are ready to start. Listen carefully. You will hear the recording twice.

Man: People always ask me why I only travel the hard way! A lot of television travel programmes are about relaxing holidays on the beach, but I've only ever made documentaries about really long trips. The last trip I did was a 50,000-mile journey around the Pacific Ocean, and it took 12 months. But then my very first trip was a 'round the world' journey, and the most difficult one was probably a car journey from the North Pole to the South Pole!

As you can imagine, I've seen a lot of the world! I'm lucky to be in really excellent health, but life is very short and I've done so much travelling that I want a change. Travelling long distances makes you extremely tired, and although it's still a great pleasure for me, I want to do something more relaxing now.

I think my next television series might be made nearer England. There's some really interesting work going on in Wales, where they've just found what remains of a 2,000-year-old town. Or I might do something about farms in France, or even cycling in Holland. There's always something to film if you look hard enough!

But I hope the programmes I've made about the really long trips will encourage other people to get on a plane and have some adventures. Some people seem to be afraid of going to a strange country and perhaps being ill there, but maybe they realise now that if I can do these trips, so can they. I'm only a very ordinary person. And obviously, you don't have to travel on your own as I always have.

I must say that until recently I hadn't ever worried about being so far from home even when the children were very small. But while I was filming in Borneo last year my wife had to have an emergency operation, and it really frightened me because I couldn't get back to England. Everything was fine in the end – but I wouldn't want to be so far away if anything like that happened to my family again.

Perhaps if I spend more time at home I can do more writing. I've done two books so far. I write about places I've seen and my feelings about them. I don't think I'll ever write fiction or poetry, but I'd be interested in writing newspaper articles. My family says I'm very difficult to live with when I'm writing at home … perhaps that's why they've never complained about me travelling!

[pause]

Now listen again.

[The recording is repeated.]

That is the end of Part 2.

[pause]

PART 3   *Now turn to Part 3, questions 14–19.*

You will hear a woman talking on the radio about an exhibition of food and cooking.
For each question, fill in the missing information in the numbered space. You now have 20 seconds to look at Part 3.

[pause]

Now we are ready to start. Listen carefully. You will hear the recording twice.

Woman: Today, I want to tell you about the Good Food Show at the Capital Exhibition Centre. There are more than 300 stands at the exhibition. I really enjoyed my visit.

First I looked at the books on sale. Jane Adams, the famous television cook, was there signing copies of her latest book. It's about making cakes so I had to have it! My family loves sweet things and I really liked her last book about making bread. There's a different famous cook there every day signing books and talking to people.

In fact, there's advice on all sorts of topics. I listened to someone from the central market talking about what you should look for when you buy fish. I've always been nervous about buying it, because how can you tell if it's really fresh? Well, I think I've got a better idea now.

Then, in the exhibition theatre, I saw a cook prepare a healthy but tasty lunch using only vegetables! They will prepare a different dish every day. Also in the theatre, at 2 o'clock every day, a cook talks about preparing delicious desserts in under 15 minutes. I tasted one made with chocolate and it was out of this world!

At the show, you can try food from all around the world, from Chile to China, and I did! I enjoyed the food from Canada most of all, although everything I tasted was really good.

The exhibition centre is open from 9 a.m. to 8 p.m. from Monday to Saturday and from 10 until 6 on Sundays. But hurry, because the last day is the 23rd of March when the Good Food Show has to make way for the Boat Show. For more details, phone …

[pause]

Now listen again.

[The recording is repeated.]

That is the end of Part 3.

[pause]

PART 4   *Now turn to Part 4, questions 20–25.*

Look at the six sentences for this part. You will hear a conversation between a teenage girl called Anna and her father about a party.
Decide if each sentence is correct or incorrect. If it is correct, put a tick in the box under A for YES. If it is not correct, put a tick in the box under B for NO. You now have 20 seconds to look at the questions for Part 4.

[pause]

Now we are ready to start. Listen carefully. You will hear the recording twice.

Girl: Are you busy Dad? I've got something I want to ask you. I've been invited to a party on Saturday. Would you give me a lift there?

Man: Where is the party then?

Girl: It's at Tom's house. His sister is 18 on Saturday, and they're having a big celebration. It's going to be brilliant. They're having a disco and Tom's Mum's a wonderful cook, so the food will be good. They've invited all their friends from school but their cousins will be there too.

Man: Well, I hope the weather stays warm so you can be outside. It sounds as if a lot of people are coming. But it all sounds fine to me. It'll be nice for you to go out at the weekend. You spend too much time at home studying. Now, what time does the party start and what time does it finish?

Girl: It starts at eight o'clock and finishes about half past twelve. But Jane's going as well, and <u>her</u> Dad will collect us and bring us home afterwards. It's all arranged.

Man: Mmm … it'll be difficult for us to <u>take</u> you. Mum and I are going to see a film which starts at 7.15. Let's see. Why don't <u>we</u> collect you and Jane at the end of the party? Then you could ask Jane's Dad to <u>take</u> you both to the party at eight.

Girl: I'm sure that'll be fine. I'll go and give Jane a ring.

Man: Just one thing though – we'll pick you up at 11.30. I really think that's late enough.

Girl: Oh Dad! That's so early. Remember we don't have to go to school on Sunday! Don't make us leave an hour before everyone else.

Man: Well, I suppose it <u>is</u> the weekend. Let's say midnight. But definitely <u>no</u> later.

Girl: But …

Man: That's my final decision! Now go and ring Jane before I change my mind!

Girl: Okay.

[pause]

Now listen again.

[The recording is repeated.]

That is the end of Part 4.

[pause]

You now have six minutes to check and copy your answers onto the answer sheet.

Note: Teacher, stop the recording here and time six minutes. Remind students when there is **one** minute remaining.

[pause]

That is the end of the test.

Sample answer sheets

Candidate Name
If not already printed, write name
in CAPITALS and complete the
Candidate No. grid (in pencil).

Candidate Signature

Examination Title

Centre

Supervisor:
If the candidate is ABSENT or has WITHDRAWN shade here ▭

Centre No.

Candidate No.

Examination
Details

0	0	0	0
1	1	1	1
2	2	2	2
3	3	3	3
4	4	4	4
5	5	5	5
6	6	6	6
7	7	7	7
8	8	8	8
9	9	9	9

PET Paper 1 Reading and Writing Candidate Answer Sheet 1

Instructions

Use a PENCIL (B or HB).

Rub out any answer you want to change with an eraser.

For **Reading:**
Mark ONE letter for each question.
For example, if you think **A** is the right answer to the
question, mark your answer sheet like this:

Part 1

1	A B C
2	A B C
3	A B C
4	A B C
5	A B C

Part 2

6	A B C D E F G H
7	A B C D E F G H
8	A B C D E F G H
9	A B C D E F G H
10	A B C D E F G H

Part 3

11	A B
12	A B
13	A B
14	A B
15	A B
16	A B
17	A B
18	A B
19	A B
20	A B

Part 4

21	A B C D
22	A B C D
23	A B C D
24	A B C D
25	A B C D

Part 5

26	A B C D
27	A B C D
28	A B C D
29	A B C D
30	A B C D
31	A B C D
32	A B C D
33	A B C D
34	A B C D
35	A B C D

Continue on the other side of this sheet ➡

S A M P L E

For **Writing (Parts 1 and 2):**

Write your answers clearly in the spaces provided.

Part 1: Write your answers below.	Do not write here
1	1 1 0
2	1 2 0
3	1 3 0
4	1 4 0
5	1 5 0

Part 2 (Question 6): Write your answer below.

Put your answer to Writing Part 3 on Answer Sheet 2 ⟶

Do not write below (Examiner use only)					
0	1	2	3	4	5

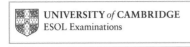

UNIVERSITY *of* **CAMBRIDGE**
ESOL Examinations

S A M P L E

Candidate Name
If not already printed, write name
in CAPITALS and complete the
Candidate No. grid (in pencil).

Candidate Signature

Examination Title

Centre

Centre No.

Candidate No.

**Examination
Details**

Supervisor:
If the candidate is ABSENT or has WITHDRAWN shade here ▭

PET Paper 1 Reading and Writing   Candidate Answer Sheet 2

Candidate Instructions:

Write your answer to Writing Part 3
on the other side of this sheet.

➡

Use a PENCIL (B or HB).

This section for use by FIRST Examiner only

Mark:

0	1.1	1.2	1.3	2.1	2.2	2.3	3.1	3.2	3.3	4.1	4.2	4.3	5.1	5.2	5.3
▭	▭	▭	▭	▭	▭	▭	▭	▭	▭	▭	▭	▭	▭	▭	▭

Examiner Number:

	0 1 2 3 4 5 6 7 8 9
	0 1 2 3 4 5 6 7 8 9
	0 1 2 3 4 5 6 7 8 9
	0 1 2 3 4 5 6 7 8 9

S A M P L E

Part 3: Mark the number of the question you are answering here ➡ Q7 or Q8
Write your answer below.

Do not write below this line

This section for use by SECOND Examiner only

Mark:

0	1.1	1.2	1.3	2.1	2.2	2.3	3.1	3.2	3.3	4.1	4.2	4.3	5.1	5.2	5.3

Examiner Number:

	0 1 2 3 4 5 6 7 8 9
	0 1 2 3 4 5 6 7 8 9
	0 1 2 3 4 5 6 7 8 9
	0 1 2 3 4 5 6 7 8 9

© UCLES/K&J Photocopiable

UNIVERSITY *of* CAMBRIDGE
ESOL Examinations

Candidate Name
If not already printed, write name
in CAPITALS and complete the
Candidate No. grid (in pencil).

Candidate Signature

Examination Title

Centre

Centre No.

Candidate No.

Examination Details

0	0	0	0
1	1	1	1
2	2	2	2
3	3	3	3
4	4	4	4
5	5	5	5
6	6	6	6
7	7	7	7
8	8	8	8
9	9	9	9

Supervisor:

If the candidate is ABSENT or has WITHDRAWN shade here ▭

PET Paper 2 Listening Candidate Answer Sheet

You must transfer all your answers from the Listening Question Paper to this answer sheet.

Instructions

Use a PENCIL (B or HB).

Rub out any answer you want to change with an eraser.

For **Parts 1, 2** and **4:**
Mark ONE letter for each question.
For example, if you think **A** is the right answer to the
question, mark your answer sheet like this:

| 0 | A̶ B̶ C |

For **Part 3:**
Write your answers clearly in the spaces next
to the numbers (14 to 19) like this:

| 0 | example |

Part 1	Part 2	Part 3	Do not write here	Part 4
1 A B C	8 A B C	14	1 14 0	20 A B
2 A B C	9 A B C	15	1 15 0	21 A B
3 A B C	10 A B C	16	1 16 0	22 A B
4 A B C	11 A B C	17	1 17 0	23 A B
5 A B C	12 A B C	18	1 18 0	24 A B
6 A B C	13 A B C	19	1 19 0	25 A B
7 A B C				

Acknowledgements

The publishers are grateful to the following for permission to reproduce copyright material. While every endeavour has been made, it has not been possible to identify the sources of all material used and in such cases the publishers would welcome information from copyright sources. Apologies are expressed for any omissions.

For permission to reproduce photographs:
CORBIS/© LWA-Sharie Kennedy p. VIII (4C); © Liz Gallivan pp. II (1B), IV (2C); Getty Images/Taxi/Harry Bartlett p. IV (2B), /PhotoDisc/Steve Mason p. VIII (4D); ImageState/Pictor p. II (1C); Impact/© Peter Arkell p. VI (3C); Photofusion/ © Gina Glover p. VI (3B), /© Crispin Hughes p. VIII (4B).

Picture clearance by Hilary Fletcher

Illustrations by Oxford Designers & Illustrators

Design concept by Peter Ducker MSTD

Cover design by Dunne & Scully

The cassettes/CDs which accompany this book were recorded at Studio AVP, London.